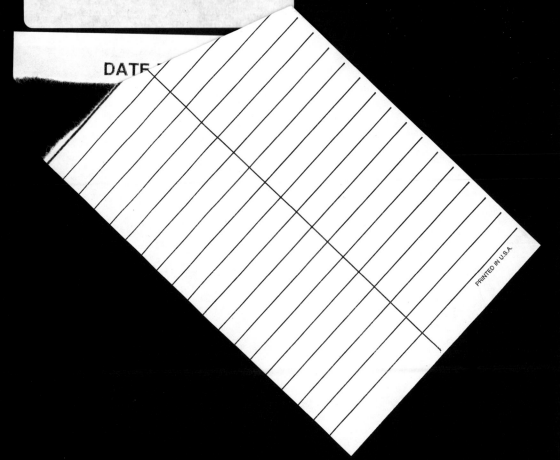

DATE

Editor: Eric Klopfer
Designers: Kris Tobiassen and Danielle Young
Production Manager: Jules Thomson

Library of Congress Cataloging-in-Publication Data

Duncan, Jody.
   The making of Avatar / Jody Duncan, Lisa Fitzpatrick.
      p. cm.
   ISBN 978-0-8109-9706-6 (alk. paper)
   1. Avatar (Motion picture : 2009) I. Fitzpatrick, Lisa. II. Title.
PN1997.2.A94D86 2010
791.43'72—dc22

2010014547

Image Credits:
Frame grab on pages 2–3 courtesy of Weta Digital.
Frame grabs on pages 29, 30, 42 (Jordu Schell), 74 (TyRuben
Ellingson), 82 (Ryan Church), 109, 111 (TOP), 128 (fight training),
128 (Cameron), 149 (BOTTOM RIGHT), 221 (Deborah Scott),
and 247 were provided courtesy of Mob Scene Productions. Photo
of Claire Prebble on page 179 courtesy of Weta Workshop. Photos
on pages 222 (BOTTOM) and 235 courtesy Stephen Rosenbaum.
Photo on page 260 courtesy of Greg Schwartz. *LIFE* magazine
photos on page 271: top two images courtesy of Jon Landau;
permission granted for bottom image by *LIFE* magazine. All other
photography by Mark Fellman on behalf of Twentieth Century
Fox and Lightstorm Entertainment.

ABRAMS
THE ART OF BOOKS SINCE 1949

115 West 18th Street
New York, NY 10011
www.abramsbooks.com

PAGES 2–3: Frame grab of Jake, Tsu'Tey, and warriors crossing to the banshee rookery; image provided courtesy of Weta Digital.

PAGES 4–5: The Venture Star (design by Procter) in orbit over Pandora; Polyphemus is in the background. Digital painting by Cole.

PAGES 6–7: Saldana during a performance-capture session with the leonopteryx in the Volume at Playa Vista, early September 2007.

PAGES 8–9: Frame grab of Neytiri teaching Jake how to shoot with a bow and arrow.

PAGES 10–11: This image is an example of Simulcam in action—the innovative technology that was created for and drove a portion of this high-tech movie production. This photograph was taken on set in the science lab section of the Ops Center, where Jake first wakes up in his avatar body. Cameron is looking into a small LCD monitor; it depicts the live-action environment with the video-game-level computer graphics (CG) character (Jake's avatar) digitally "composited" into the virtual version of the room that Cameron, the camera operator, and the "MedTech" actors physically occupy. Worthington's performance-capture shoot was conducted earlier that day (in another part of Stone Street Studios in Wellington). In the background, the stereo camera rig (configured on a Steadicam) composes an angle as directed by Cameron. Due to the wonders of Simulcam, Cameron sees this as a real-time video composite of the current live-action view combined with the previously captured performance by Worthington as Jake's avatar. Cameron then directs the action as if Jake's avatar coexists in the same environment as the live-action MedTechs (December 2007).

ACKNOWLEDGMENTS

JODY DUNCAN: I would like to thank publisher and friend Don Shay, first and foremost, for granting access to interview material originally gathered for *Cinefex* magazine. It was invaluable. Thanks to Jon Landau, Eric Himmel, and Debbie Olshan for their role in putting this project together, and to Abrams's Eric Klopfer for helping me to see it to its end. Thank you, Eric Roth, for providing me with essential materials. Thanks to Lisa Fitzpatrick for taking on the huge task of gathering images and then writing the captions for those images. Finally, I am most profoundly grateful for the memory of Staci Della-Rocco, who saw everyone.

LISA FITZPATRICK: Thank you to Eric Himmel of Abrams and to Jon Landau, as well as Virginia King and Debbie Olshan from FOX, for supporting my participation in this project. Thank you also to the many artists and companies who made time and provided additional artwork—all of which has greatly enriched this book—including: Weta Digital, Wayne Barlowe, Neville Page, Ryan Church, John Rosengrant, Steven Messing, Dylan Cole, TyRuben Ellingson, Yuri Bartoli, and Stan Winston Studio. Thanks to Ben Procter for his faithful commitment to getting the facts straight and to all for their consistent patience and good humor during my many follow-up questions and requests, including Chrissy Quesada and Andrea Sticht from the FOX stills department and Natasha Turner of Weta Digital. Special appreciation goes to project consultant Stephen Rosenbaum for providing numerous technical explanations as well as to Rick Carter and Robert Stromberg for their support and insights. Much appreciation goes to Stephen Rivkin for your time and the last minute "save"; thanks to Jason Gaudio, Chris Marino, and to Tom Grane, principal at Mob Scene for generously making staff and materials available, including his many interview transcripts for the manuscript. LEI's Billy Barnhart was invaluable throughout production; thanks as well to Reymundo Perez for your time early on. Gratitude goes to Eric Klopfer, Danielle Young, and Ivy McFadden of Abrams, as well as to designer Kris Tobiassen, for their endurance, and to Jody Duncan, for producing such a well-crafted manuscript.

These images were part of the *Avatar* global press tour covered by *LIFE* magazine. **LEFT**: Saldana and Weaver in Russia (photo by Landau). **BELOW, TOP**: Saldana explores the cockpit during the global press tour (photo by Landau). **BELOW, BOTTOM**: Cameron, Weaver, Lang, Saldana, and Worthington assemble on the tarmac in Berlin.

THE MAKING OF
AVATAR

Jody Duncan and Lisa Fitzpatrick

ABRAMS, NEW YORK

CONTENTS

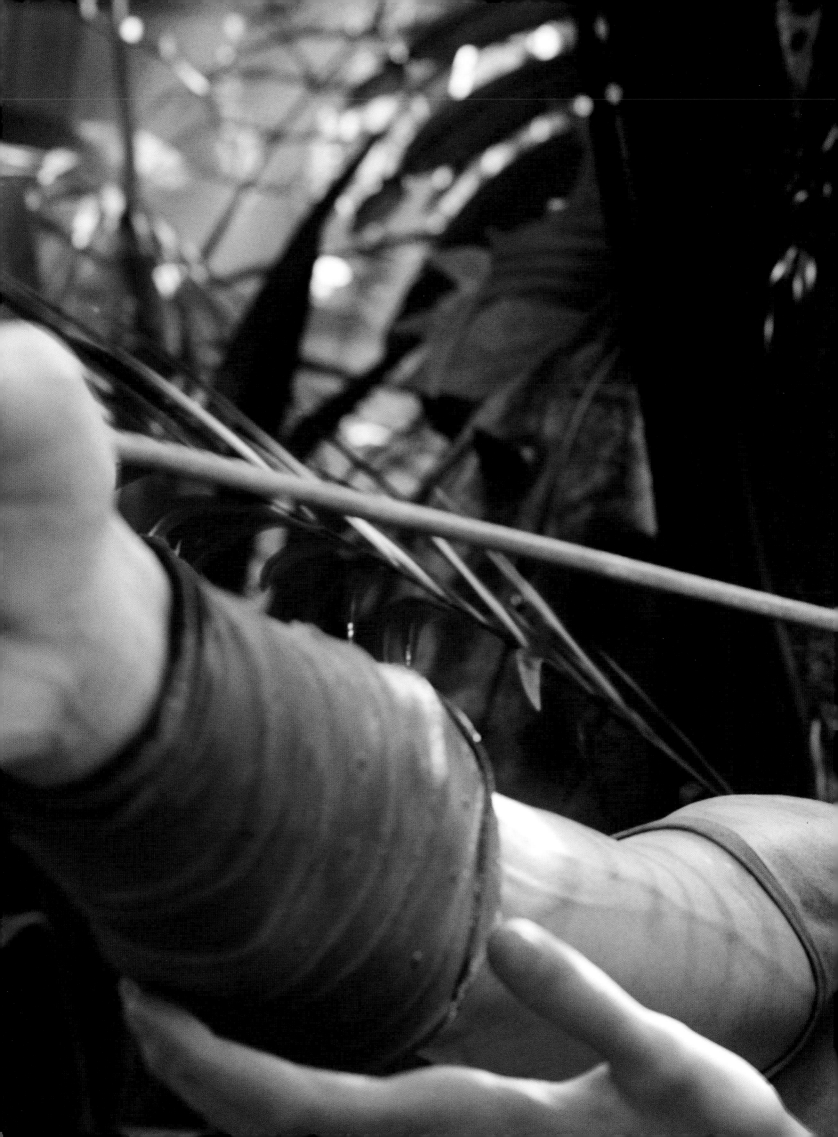

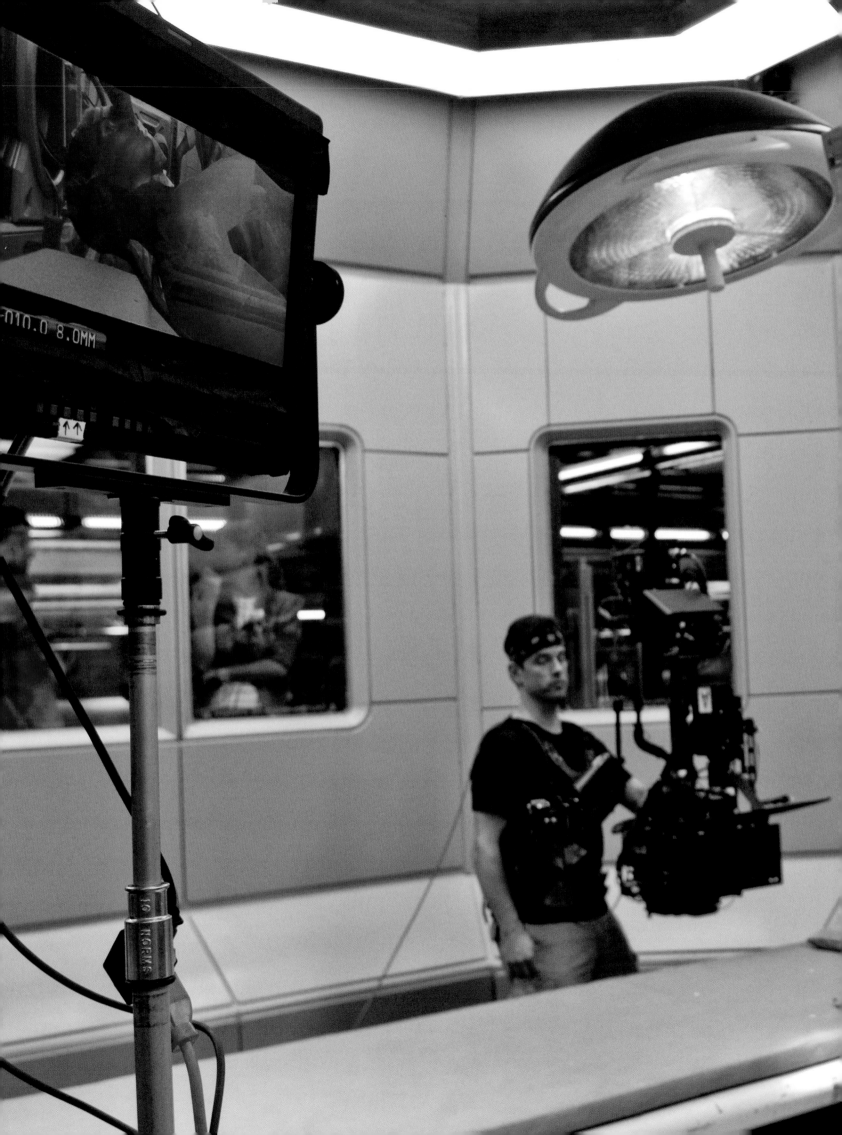

ONE

SNGÄ'IKRR: BEGINNING

The only way of discovering the limits of the possible is to venture a little way past them into the impossible.

—ARTHUR C. CLARKE'S SECOND LAW OF
SCIENTIFIC AND TECHNOLOGICAL PREDICTION

Sometime in the late 1970s in Orange County, California, James Cameron painted a picture of a tall, slender blue girl standing in a field of magenta grass. It was an image Cameron, still years away from directing his first feature film, never could have realized on screen at the time. The technology to create this otherworldly, cyan-colored girl didn't exist yet. And wouldn't for some 30 years.

The time-consuming, endurance-testing nature of covering an actor in prosthetics is the stuff of movie lore. Lon Chaney Jr.'s makeup for his title role in 1941's *The Wolf Man* required six hours to apply and three hours to remove, making for a nine-hour workday before a single frame had been committed to film. During production of the 1968 *Planet of the Apes*, rubber-encased actors suffered dangerously elevated body temperatures while shooting in Arizona's hundred-degree temperatures, and had to drink liquefied meals through a straw during the shoot so as not to disturb makeup master John Chambers's ape masks. Prosthetic materials and techniques had improved somewhat by the time Jim Carrey played the title role in 2000's *How the Grinch Stole Christmas*, but the transformation of the actor into the Dr. Seuss character

OPPOSITE: James Cameron's original sketch upon which the final look for Neytiri and all the Na'vi was based. Although a bank of artists explored numerous variations over the course of many months, ultimately they returned to many of the very specific, core features embedded in this early depiction.

still involved three hours in the makeup chair every day. The confinement of the latex skin and furry suit was so unbearable for Carrey, he enlisted a Navy SEAL to teach him torture-resistance techniques as a coping mechanism. In addition to its tendency to slow down production and make for irritable actors, the suits-and-prosthetics approach has other constraints. Characters can be only so tall, and can move only according to the performer's physiology and the restrictions of the suit. Also, no matter how artfully designed and applied, prosthetics increase the mass of the actor's face, which limits the range of looks that can be achieved. You could give Danny De-Vito a *bigger* nose as the Penguin in *Batman Returns* (1992), but there was no way to make his nose smaller.

Despite the many downsides of prosthetics and suits, filmmakers continued to use them, because they were the only means through which actors could portray fantasy

characters of the humanoid kind. Stop-motion animation, full-scale puppets, animatronics, and, later, computer animation were all fine for realizing robots, monsters, dinosaurs, and aliens with a limited emotional range, but for the first one hundred years of cinema, if filmmakers wanted to create a fantasy character of some complexity, a character with spirit, heart, and soul, they needed a complex human being with spirit, heart, and soul to play it. They needed an actor.

The question of how to create emotionally complex fantasy characters was very much on James Cameron's mind in 1995, even as he prepared to go into production on *Titanic*. That year, the writer/director had written a treatment titled *Avatar*, intended as a cutting-edge project for Digital Domain, the visual-effects company he'd founded in 1993 with effects master Stan Winston.

The eighty-page treatment mapped out the entire world of *Avatar* and included all the film's creatures, environments, and characters, plus quite a few more that wouldn't make the cut a decade later when the script was written. In the treatment, Jake Sully was "Josh Sully," Neytiri was "Zuleika," and the thanator was called the "manticore"—but aside from these minor deviations, the treatment recounted the story just as it would play out in the final movie.

Josh (Jake) is a paraplegic former Marine who replaces his dead twin brother in the avatar program on distant Pandora, a moon that orbits the gas giant Polyphemus in the Alpha Centauri-A star system.

Pandora is a densely forested environment resplendent with exotic plant life, massive trees, and mountains of floating rock held aloft by a powerful magnetic field. Scientists working for the Earth-based Resources Development Administration (RDA)—which has established a base on Pandora to mine a precious superconductor mineral called, colloquially, "unobtainium"—have overcome the problem of the moon's toxic atmosphere by combining human DNA with that of the indigenous Na'vi people. The resulting avatar, controlled by the original human via a consciousness-link machine, is able to move about Pandora without the aid of cumbersome breathing devices.

As an avatar, Josh is assigned a covert mission to infiltrate a Na'vi tribe and learn their ways so that RDA forces might persuade them to leave a forested area that has been the clan's home for millennia—an area that, unfortunately for the tribe, is rich in unobtainium. In fulfilling that mission, Josh's loyalties gradually shift from the RDA to the

Na'vi, as he learns to love their princess, Neytiri, their culture, and their way of life. When the RDA security forces implement plans to destroy the clan's ancestral home, Josh leads a low-tech battle against the aggressors, driving them from Pandora and saving the Na'vi homeland.

Avatar was inspired by Cameron's love of the "stranger in a strange land" narratives of Edgar Rice Burroughs's *John Carter of Mars* (1964) and Rudyard Kipling's *The Man Who Would Be King* (1888), both favorite stories of his youth. "I wanted to create a familiar type of adventure in an unfamiliar environment," Cameron explained, "by setting the classic tale of a newcomer to a foreign land and culture on an alien planet. I'd dreamed of creating a film like this, set on another world of great danger and beauty, since I was a kid reading pulp science fiction and comic books by the truckload, and sitting in math class drawing creatures and aliens behind my propped-up textbook. So I'd been thinking about a lot of ideas for a long time, and *Avatar* almost wrote itself in about two weeks."

From the beginning, Cameron had known that the alien Na'vi, as he envisioned them, were far too outlandish to be portrayed by actors in suits or prosthetic makeup. In the treatment, he had described the prototypical Na'vi as:

[B]igger than a human. It would stand about ten feet tall. Its skin is blue, two shades of blue in a banded pattern like a snake or a lizard, though the skin is smooth, not scaly. An iridescent cyan blue, almost robin's egg, is contrasted by deep ultramarine, which borders purple. The darker color is almost solid on the back and down the back of the legs. The body is strangely human in most ways. The waist is narrow and elongated. The shoulders are very wide, giving a V-shaped upper back. The neck is long, maybe twice as long as the average human, or a little longer than some *Vogue* models. And we will see it can turn almost 180 degrees, like an owl. The body overall is more slender proportionally than the average human, reminiscent of a Masai or Watusi. The musculature is sharply defined, giving no sense of emaciation despite the thin proportions.

In other words, the Na'vi were the embodiment of human wish fulfillment: taller, more slender, more muscular, and more athletically gifted than any human being could be—or than any human actor in makeup could portray.

Cameron's idea at the time he wrote the treatment was that he would shoot live-action plates representing Pan-

Costume design sketch (**OPPOSITE**) and an early variation on Neytiri's face (**ABOVE**) by Cameron.

dora's rain forests and then populate them with computer-animated Na'vi and avatars. Steven Spielberg had used the same technique, with great success, for *Jurassic Park* just two years earlier, augmenting Stan Winston Studio's practical dinosaur puppets with computer-animated dinosaurs that were composited into live-action plates shot in Hawaii and on stage sets.

But computer-animating dinosaurs was one thing; computer-animating *Avatar*'s Na'vi would be something else. As groundbreaking as the achievement was, *Jurassic Park* had managed to get by with only fifty-five computer-animated-dinosaur shots, whereas the Na'vi would be major characters in *Avatar*, prominently featured in the majority of its scenes. More importantly, the T. rex and velociraptors of Spielberg's film were beasts with a limited range of expression, whereas the Na'vi would be intelligent, speaking, feeling beings—beings that could only be brought to full emotional life by actors.

Cameron's hope was that, through emerging motion-capture technology, he would be able to capture actors' performances and then transpose them onto computer-generated characters. In 1995, motion capture was a fairly new, but functional, technique within the film industry, and it works today much as it did then. Actors wear black Lycra suits dotted with "markers," small spheres covered with retro-reflective film called Scotchlite—the same remarkable material that makes a stop sign light up brightly in your headlights. The actors perform in a capture zone called the "Volume," a stage area surrounded by scores of black-and-

white video cameras. Each camera emits infrared light that reflects off the markers and back to the source, so it sees the markers brightly in an otherwise black field.

The resulting image is a moving swarm of dots, and each camera's dots are slightly different, based on the different angles of view. The computer analyzes all the dot clouds and "solves" in a matter of microseconds for each actor's body position, and this solve is updated sixty times per second.

The solve yields a skeleton, which in turn is used to "drive" or animate a computer-generated (CG) character. In real time, as the actors move, their characters move identically in the virtual world, gesture for gesture. By recording the swarms of dots, the motion is "captured," and can then be edited, refined, combined with backgrounds and other virtual elements, and then played back days or even months later, to bring the actors' performances back to life.

While motion capture had proved successful in capturing gross body movement at the time Cameron conceived

Avatar, it hadn't advanced to the point where it could capture the subtleties of an actor's *facial* performance—every slight quiver of a lip, raising of a brow, or flaring of a nostril; all the minute firings of the nervous system, the twitches of the muscles, and the movement of skin and bone that go into human expression. What Cameron would need for *Avatar* wasn't just motion capture, but rather "emotion" capture, a way to retain an actor's performance—in all of its emotionality and complexity—in his CG Na'vi and avatars.

In no way was he advocating that CG characters *replace* actors. On the contrary, what he was proposing would *empower* them. Through their CG counterparts, actors would be able to portray a limitless range of exotic characters—characters of any age, any gender, and any species. The transfer of a human performance to a CG character would be, essentially, the twenty-first-century version of prosthetics, but without the design restrictions, the excruciating hours in a makeup chair, or the discomforts of performing under layers of latex.

Curious as to whether, with enough effort, current motion-capture technology could be advanced into the realm of true *performance* capture, Cameron conducted some rudimentary facial-capture tests at Digital Domain, using the data to drive the animation of simple Na'vi computer models. "The Na'vi we tested were much more alien than they ended up being in the movie," recalled *Avatar* animation director Andy Jones, one of those animators at Digital Domain who tested the concept—and who still has the crew T-shirt to prove it. "Later, Jim realized that they would have to be more human-like in order for people to relate to them."

The tests, while promising, proved unequivocally that facial-capture technology had a long, long way to go before it would produce the type of expressive, emotional fantasy character Cameron had in mind for *Avatar*. "Despite wanting to push the technology," Cameron said, "when we really evaluated it, we felt like we were too many steps away from being able to do it—years away. Within a single pro-

duction, we wouldn't be able to push it that hard or that far, no matter how much money we threw at it. So I said, 'Okay, fine, the timing's off,' threw the script in the back of a stack of files, and that was that."

With the future *Avatar* project now on the back burner, Cameron turned his undivided attention to *Titanic*, a monumental production that would consume all of his time and energies for the next two years. *Titanic's* production would be extraordinarily demanding, both physically and logistically, requiring Cameron and his crews to replicate, in detail, many areas of the real ship in full-scale, flood those sets with millions of gallons of water, and shoot a full-scale sinking ship at a new oceanfront Fox Studio in Mexico built especially for the production. Cameron had endured physical trials even before the start of principal photography, when he'd made a series of North Atlantic dives in small Russian submersibles to shoot the real *Titanic* on the ocean floor, acquiring footage that would make its way into the film.

After *Titanic*'s phenomenal, record-breaking release, there was much speculation as to what Cameron could possibly do for an encore, but rather than rush to fulfill those expectations, he continued to explore the ocean deep, shooting stereoscopic underwater footage with the Fusion 3D camera system he had developed with digital-camera co-designer Vince Pace. That footage became the core of Cameron's two 3-D documentaries: *Ghosts of the Abyss* (2003), which further explored the *Titanic* wreckage, and *Aliens of the Deep* (2005), which showcased, in three-dimensional splendor, exotic life forms in the mid-ocean ridge system.

While allowing Cameron to indulge the explorer/scientist side of his nature, these underwater filming expeditions also helped him to grow as a filmmaker in ways that would prove critical to *Avatar*'s production. "The ocean hasn't read your script," Cameron commented. "You go out there and whatever happens, happens, and your technology has to work because there are no second takes. You can't just fix it in [postproduction]. It has to actually work, and there is a rigor and discipline to that work from which I learned a lot. The thing that I learned the most was the necessity to build and manage a team; and as a filmmaker, I don't think I was very good at that before. I think I'm really good at it now, and it comes out of those expeditions."

Making the 3-D documentaries was also an opportunity to refine the 3-D camera system, which Cameron knew he would one day employ for a stereoscopic feature film. "Jim is a person who does his craft as an art," noted *Avatar* producer and longtime Cameron collaborator Jon Landau. "And art needs inspiration. Coming off of *Titanic*, Jim's search for inspiration went into exploration—exploration of the oceans, but also exploration of the 3-D medium that ultimately serviced *Avatar*. With Jim, everything is a stepping-stone. He's always looking beyond."

Cameron's entire film career, in fact, had been an exercise in looking beyond. When developing *The Abyss* (1989), he had included a scene in which a watery pseudopod moves through an underwater oil rig, comes face-to-face with Mary Elizabeth Mastrantonio's character, and then mimics her expressions as she watches, spellbound. Cameron had conceived the pseudopod—realized by Industrial Light & Magic (ILM) through computer graphics—specifically as a means of testing whether ILM would be able to produce the CG, liquid-metal terminator he had in mind for *Terminator 2* (1991). "Jim knew that if he

couldn't solve it for *The Abyss*, he couldn't make *T2* happen," said Landau.

Similarly, Cameron had looked beyond when he made *Titanic*, implementing early motion-capture technology not only to populate the ship with digital background passengers, but also to investigate how he might use the technology for the creation of synthetic characters and creatures in a future feature film.

In the eight post-*Titanic* years that Cameron spent exploring the ocean, making his documentaries and developing other projects, there were incremental advancements in the technology that elevated simple motion capture to something much closer to true performance capture. Performance capture became an exciting new filmmaking tool that sparked a number of projects by enthusiasts such as director Robert Zemeckis, who had Tom Hanks don a motion-capture suit to play multiple CG characters in *The Polar Express*. But it wasn't until Cameron saw the emotionally compelling, nuanced performance of the computer-generated Gollum—performed on set by Andy Serkis and then realized by Weta Digital—in Peter Jackson's *The Lord of the Rings* that he took notice and considered that, perhaps, performance-capture technology had finally caught up to his vision for *Avatar*.

Cameron and Landau had been encouraged about the prospects of the technology even before seeing Gollum. In 2002, Cameron's Lightstorm Entertainment production company had conducted its own facial-performance-capture test for a project called *Brother Termite*. "We shot a whole scene," Jon Landau recalled, "a walk-and-talk between a live-action woman and a CGI [computer-generated imagery] character. We used image-based technology where an actor wore a head-rigged camera to gather the images of his face." Using those cameras, image-based facial-capture software tracked the surface movement of the actor's face and streamed that facial movement to a CG head displayed on a computer monitor. ILM then completed the scene in two ways: In one version, ILM animators used the facial-capture data to animate the CG character; in another, they keyframe-animated the character. The results of the comparison test were obvious: The performance-capture animation more closely matched the original actor performance—and it would provide Cameron with the means through which he could create his Na'vi and avatar characters in *Avatar*.

PREVIOUS SPREAD: Wide view of the performance-capture stage, also referred to as "the Volume," at Playa Vista in Los Angeles. This photograph was taken from the second floor, a place Cameron dubbed "the lab," where the production's in-house visual effects team worked.

ABOVE: Cameron shoots live action for *Avatar* of recently landed SecOps troops running through the jungle (Stone Street Studios, Wellington, New Zealand, late January 2008). The Fusion 3-D camera was the result of seven years of development between Cameron and Vince Pace.

By 2005—ten years since Cameron had conceived *Avatar*—not only had performance capture come a long way, so too had 3-D technology. Through the making of the 3-D underwater documentaries, Cameron and Vince Pace had significantly advanced both the stereoscopic process and the quality of the final imagery. Cameron was ready to take it out and see what it could do on a full-length feature film, but his initial impulse was a cautious one. In conversation with his good friend and collaborator

Stan Winston—creator of the Terminator robots—Cameron had mentioned that he thought he'd try out the new 3-D technology on a smaller film first. Winston, never one to think small, wouldn't hear of it. He convinced Cameron that if he was going to bet on a 3-D feature film, he should go all-in with his biggest, most ambitious project. That project was *Avatar*.

Given the still-nascent performance-capture technology that would have to be developed, Cameron and Jon

Landau knew they were looking at an epic project that would require large sums of money and years of effort. They would be pushing a very large boulder up a very high, steep mountain, and so, rather than jump immediately into preproduction, Cameron and Landau made a pitch to Twentieth Century Fox, asking the studio to put up $10 million solely for the purposes of technological and conceptual development. Using those funds, Cameron and Landau would set up technical and artistic teams to explore *Avatar*'s feasibility, and at the end of that development phase, Fox would either pass or give the production a green light. Either way, Fox's investment would be amortized through future projects employing the technologies Cameron's team would develop.

The studio accepted the deal, and Cameron and Landau soon after set up studio space for technology development at Playa Vista, a film-production complex on the west side of Greater Los Angeles that was once the home of Hughes Aircraft. Concurrently, the filmmakers hired four concept artists—Wayne Barlowe, Yuri Bartoli, Jordu Schell, and Neville Page—to develop artwork illustrating the world of Pandora, specifically its varieties of exotic and alien creatures. CG artist Robert Powers was also brought on to develop motion studies of those creatures.

The artists were told precious little about the top-secret project when they came on. All they knew was that, unlike so many films based on comic books, graphic novels, and other known quantities, this one required the creation of an entire world from scratch. "Jim just told us that he was creating an epic science-fiction film and that we had to inhabit this world with flora and fauna—all manner of living creatures," Jordu Schell recalled. "He wanted them to be very convincing and realistic, but he also wanted us to come up with a variety of life forms that no one had ever seen before. Jim was very specific about that. He didn't want any of this to look like something that had been done before."

In the beginning, the artists worked in what Cameron only half-jokingly referred to as his "man cave," a dwelling next door to his home in Malibu that he had purchased specifically as a workspace. Though he was often out of town on diving expeditions for the first three months, Cameron—an accomplished artist who had worked as an art director early in his film career—would join the artists in the Malibu annex when he was in Los Angeles, sitting at large art tables and sketching with them. To inspire the team, Cameron occasionally brought out underwater photographs he had taken of colorful, unusual marine life, or paintings and sketches he had rendered for his previous films, such as *Aliens* (1986) and *The Abyss*.

Initially working mostly with pencil and paper, the artists spent months drawing concepts for Pandora's creatures, all of which were described in vivid language in Cameron's treatment. As fantastic as these animals would be, Cameron insisted that they have some basis in the natural sciences. His invented names for the creatures—the "hammerhead titanothere," the "thanator," the "leonopteryx," and others—were derived from Latin and Greek word origins, as are real species names. "Thanator" came from the archaic Greek *thantos*, meaning "death," and "leonopteryx" combined Greek words for lion and wing. In the same vein, Cameron encouraged the concept artists to work from accurate science drawings of extinct species in creating their designs. "We took a lot of inspiration from those illustrations," said Yuri Bartoli. "Everything was based on real-life biology, which Jim knows a lot about. Being able to discuss the science behind all of these animals with him helped us to produce better designs."

The artists were still free to let their imaginations roam, however, and to search for inspiration in unlikely arenas. "There came a time," Wayne Barlowe recalled, "when I wanted to push the designers toward something more extreme. I didn't want to show Jim what I thought would be creatures that were *too* conventional." Early on, the artists actually played with concepts that had an automotive design influence, and they produced rounds of auto-inspired drawings. "I was very interested in Formula One cars. So we came up with designs that combined the smooth skin of poison-dart frogs with a kind of cetacean set of lines, and melded that with the strange dynamic forms of Formula One cars. Those cars have lines that are very flowing and graceful, and there are also detail lines on them that are meant to be aerodynamic. It's a short jump to go from that to looking at the more hydrodynamic lines that whales have. So we looked at how nature might incorporate some of those lines, and we started to come up with things that looked very alien. It was a way to get away from the more standardized terrestrial forms." The designs, ultimately, moved in a different direction, but some creatures would retain remnants of this auto-design phase, such as breathing mechanisms that looked like air-intake valves.

A notion Cameron entertained from the earliest stages of design was that Pandora's creatures would have six

limbs, rather than four. "We wanted all of the designs to be unique to our world," explained Jon Landau. "We didn't want any confusion that, 'Oh, I might have seen that in another movie.' So all of our creatures are six-limbed, something you haven't seen."

The concept artists, upon first hearing the idea, were not certain that a six-legged creature was something that *should* be seen. "Jim not only wanted six limbs," recalled Neville Page, "he wanted front paws on some of the creatures that would be almost like human hands. And that scared me. There was a lot of stuff Jim threw at us at the beginning that I didn't quite see. He'd had ten years on us to see it. We'd just had the first couple of hours reading the treatment, and thinking: 'Hands? Real human hands on a six-legged creature? Oh, Jim, I don't know. Do I tell him? Do you want to tell him, Jordu?' There were so many times when I thought, 'I don't get it.'"

Though Cameron liked the six-limbed idea for its novelty, he rejected novelty for its own sake in the design of any creature—or anything else—in the world of Pandora.

Throughout the design effort, Cameron stressed again and again that there had to be scientific logic to the fanciful concepts, including that of a six-legged creature. A plausible purpose for the extra pair of limbs, from an evolutionary standpoint, became the subject of many discussions between Cameron and the artists, and they finally determined that Pandora's dense, overgrown jungle and massive trees provided sufficient justification, as the extra limbs would enable the creatures to hold on to their prey while climbing trees or maintaining a secure four-legged footing on the uneven terrain. To ensure that a six-limbed animal could move with some grace, CG artist Robert Powers generated motion studies that were later extrapolated into six-legged walk and run cycles by ILM animator Paul Kavanagh.

The first six-legged creature that would appear on-screen for any length of time was the massive hammerhead that Jake encounters in his initial foray into the forest as an avatar. Yuri Bartoli was primarily responsible for the design of this armored, rhinoceros-like hammerhead, so

ABOVE: Cameron on the live action set at Stone Street Studios in Wellington, New Zealand (mid-February 2008), directing the scene in which the defeated humans are leaving Pandora. The ten-foot-tall Na'vi models (created by Stan Winston Studio) were used for eye-lines of the cast as they walked by.

named due to the large anvil-shaped bone structure at the front of its head. In the scene, the hammerhead retreats with the appearance of the thanator, Pandora's version of the "king of the jungle." Cameron had described the thanator in his treatment as "a black, six-limbed panther from hell, the size of a tractor trailer . . . with a venomous striking tail and a massive, armored jaw lined with nine-inch fangs." Each of the four original *Avatar* concept artists offered illustrations of the thanator as they struggled to find just the right look—and that struggle would continue well beyond the concept-design phase.

Separated from his group in his escape from the thanator, Jake spends a night alone in the forest, stalked and then attacked by a pack of "viperwolves." Cameron's treatment described these predators as "sleek, muscular creature[s] with multiple rows of sharp teeth; hairless, with shiny skin that looks like leather armor, mostly black but banded with vermilion and thin lines of iridescent blue; bright, intelligent green eyes, with glistening fangs that look as if they could be made of glass."

There would be many iterations of the viperwolf's design, but the driving concepts of shiny, hairless, leather armor, glassy fangs, and iridescent red and blue bands were never abandoned. There were endless discussions about the nature of the armor, how thick it was to be, how rigid or flexible, and how it would overlap. Too thick and it became crablike; too thin and the skin lacked detail and looked like molded plastic. The references the team fastened on finally were the overlapping segment of a shrimp's tail, or the overlapping scales on a snake's underbelly, both of which form smooth, flexible surfaces from thin, overlapping sheets.

ABOVE: The prolemuris swings from limb to limb in its native Pandoran environment. Seen for only a few seconds early in the film, the monkey-like prolemuris (designed by lead creature designer Neville Page) establishes the genealogical connection between the six-legged creatures and the more humanoid, four-limbed Na'vi. The lateral membranes beneath their arms allow the wind to catch their fall as they drop from canopy to canopy in the multitiered forest.

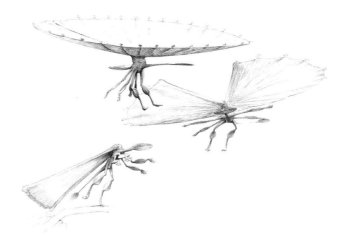

ABOVE: Initial creature concept designer Wayne Barlowe's study of the fan lizard—colored pencil over a photocopy of the original drawing. As with many other creatures, "Jim had a very specific concept for the fan lizard's structure and movement," notes Barlowe. "It was simply a case of visually realizing it."

ABOVE: Barlowe's motion study (designed to demonstrate the script's analogy of an opening and closing Chinese paper fan) revealing the take-off mechanics of the fan lizard as requested by Jon Landau.

Cameron saw the viperwolf as having a mix of doglike and simian characteristics, with the loping stride of a wolf transitioning to the climbing of an ape as it moved up onto the tree limbs overhead via the grasping of its nearly human hands. The artists studied mink and weasels, as well, to give the creature a slinking, undulating quality that was unlike the gait produced by the relatively stiff spine of a dog.

The artists also produced multitudinous sketches of the "banshee," a flying creature with a thirty-eight-foot wingspan that lives in the mountainous regions of Pandora. Through neural fibers at the tip of a long, braidlike queue, every young Na'vi hunter bonds for life with a specific banshee, a sacred connection demonstrated in the scene in which Jake climbs to a mountaintop rookery to claim one of the creatures for his own. Though the banshee was similar in concept to a dragon or a pterodactyl, Cameron challenged the artists to design a creature unlike any seen in previous fantasy films. "We've seen this *type* of thing many times before," admitted Bartoli, "but we wanted to take it in a new direction."

As always, the artists looked to nature for inspiration, referencing footage and photographs of bats to study how the leathery membranes of their wings flutter between rigid riblike structures, how blood vessels pulse through translucent areas of the membrane, and how their facial features are structured. The artists incorporated those fea-

tures into early banshee drawings, but continued to refine the design for many, many months. They spent more time on the banshee design, in fact, than they would on any other creature. "The banshee was a real exercise in evolution," said Neville Page.

As he had with all the creatures, Cameron urged the artists to find "the metaphor." What did the creature represent in the story? What was being conveyed at a subconscious level? The struggle, always, was to combine the alien and the familiar: Every creature had to resonate with the audience in some recognizable way, and yet the details of the animal had to constantly remind the viewer that he was in an alien world, seeing an animal he'd never seen or imagined before.

The metaphor for the banshee was "bird of prey." Hawks, eagles and other raptors were studied for form and movement. A familiar feature of eagles, condors, and other soaring hunters is the array of splayed "primary feathers" at the wing tips, which move subtly to adjust the bird's flight path. This observation led to the creation of the banshee's "primary vanes," the transparent structures that form the outer wing. To differentiate them from the feathers of a terrestrial bird, they were reimagined as vanes formed like individual dragonfly wings—transparent membranes made rigid by veinlike structures. This was the alien feature. And yet, the way in which they fan open to catch

the air as the banshee takes flight or move subtly to adjust their soaring glide is familiar to anyone who has ever watched a hawk in flight.

A lot of time was spent, both in the design phase and later during animation, on the flight dynamics of the banshee. It was decided that the banshee would have four wings, and that the aft wings, also called the canards, would have a dual function. Sometimes they would act much like a bird's tail feathers, for steering, especially in very tight, high-performance turns. But when the banshee needed power to climb, or to fly rapidly when being pursued, the canards would flap like the main wings, in deep power strokes. Since there was no analog to this on Earth, considerable testing was required to create flap cycles that looked natural. The exact way in which the primary vanes folded and the wings furled upon landing took some time to work out. The creature was exceedingly complex in motion, having the ability to land and take off from vertical cliff faces, horizontal branches, and flat ground. Each one of these landing and takeoff scenarios required a different approach. The banshee also had a single steering vane at the base of its splayed primary vanes, called the allula,

which ended in a large scythelike claw used in hunting and for grasping during landing.

One of the banshee features that required many redesigns was its jaw and surrounding mouth area, which Cameron envisioned articulating in a very complex, multiaxial manner, due to an extra bone along the jawline. When the banshee shrieked, its bifurcated mouth would pull back and reveal its rows of teeth. Inspiration for the final jaw structures came from two sources: venomous snakes and barracuda. The snake can rotate its fangs forward through ninety degrees, from a stowed position when the mouth is closed, to the striking position. This principle led to the creation of a "quadrate bone" that racked the entire row of glassy fangs forward as the banshee's mouth opened wide. This was combined with the maxilla of a barracuda, to create a mouth that was decidedly fishlike. "The conceit here," said Cameron, "was that the banshee had evolved not from land-dwelling reptiles, as the pterodactyls had on Earth, but from flying fish." The banshee's folding teeth created the opportunity to portray the creature in a variety of moods. When provoked, it could be ferocious, baring dagger-like fangs; but

ABOVE: A very early design effort by Barlowe of what was first referred to as the manticore (and later became the thanator). A hammerhead titanothere, designed by supervising visual art director Yuri Bartoli, charges in the background.

when it was docile, the fangs would be concealed and it would seem more birdlike, taking its food gently from Neytiri with a seemingly toothless mouth that was more like a beak.

Cameron had described the leonopteryx, a flying predator with an eighty-foot wingspan, as the king predator of the air, feeding on banshees and "munching them like salted peanuts. . . . When it plummets out of the sky in a full-delta tuck like a hawk swooping, it is called the 'last shadow'—because it's the last thing you'll ever see before it kills you." From the beginning, the designers had rendered the leonopteryx as a vividly colored creature. "There were a number of underpinning philosophies that Jim wanted to see implemented," said Wayne Barlowe, "and one of them was a notion that these creatures would have insanely vibrant colors."

Many competing designs for the leonopteryx emerged, but the artists found themselves returning to an early drawing by Wayne Barlowe, which showed a creature with an enormous blue crest projecting both above and below its head, forming an axelike shape. This crest became the signature element of the leonopteryx design, right through to its final stages. The "leo," as it was known, was to have four wings, but their design and function were very different from those of the banshee because the leo would also have legs with powerful grasping claws, like an eagle. In fact, the "metaphor" for the leonopteryx was the eagle, a noble and powerful lone predator, both majestic and fearsome. Because Jake's bonding with the leonopteryx was such an important plot point, the leo had to be a character as much as a creature design. Its final visage is scarred from many epic aerial battles, and its eyes are piercing and intelligent, perhaps even wise.

The leonopteryx plays a crucial role in the Na'vi defeat of the RDA's military forces in the end battle, as does the "direhorse," a large blue-and-gold armored equine creature that serves as the Na'vi warriors' mount. As with the banshee, the Na'vi bond with the direhorse, enabling rider and beast to move together with symbiotic ease. Just as he had with the leonopteryx, Wayne Barlowe created one seminal sketch that "cracked" the direhorse design. With a few economical lines, he captured the "essence" of a horse with a gestural crest and head shape that were nevertheless quite alien in their details. The trifurcated hoof design was based on the earliest horse fossils found on Earth, the Eohippus. What emerged from this design process was an animal both noble and fearsome, unmistakably horselike and yet decidedly alien. Though it had the size and power of a dinosaur, it fed like a hummingbird on the nectar of flowers with its meter-long tongue.

Though it would be seen only briefly, the gazelle-like hexapede was subjected to the same artistic care as the most prominently featured beasts. "Even for a background creature like the hexapede," said Neville Page, "Jim went [over] it with a fine-tooth comb. There wasn't one background creature where he just said, 'Anything, I don't care, just give me anything.' Every single element of every creature was thought out, literally, head to toe."

The "prolemuris" is seen in only a single scene, swinging through the trees and then turning full face to the camera. Despite its brief appearance, the monkeylike creature serves an important function in the film, as it provides the evolutionary link between Pandora's six-limbed creatures and the four-limbed Na'vi. "By having this other ape-like creature," said Page, who designed the prolemuris, "it shows there's an evolutionary branching that occurred. My challenge was to say, 'If we have hexapedal creatures on this planet and we've got the Na'vi with no evidence of having six limbs, can we show that there's a transition, evolutionarily speaking?'" That transition is illustrated in the creature's front limbs, which are bifurcated up to the "elbow" point and then merge into one appendage. This created the evolutionary bridge between the Pandoran primates and the more highly evolved Na'vi. Interestingly, the only other four-limbed creatures on the planet are the four-winged banshees. The other flying creatures— the tetrapterons, leonopteryx, and the stingbats (seen only in the extended theatrical re-release)—all have six limbs, inclusive of their four wings.

Page also designed the "fan lizard," which is first seen as a rather ugly, toady creature, but which then, at night, lifts into the air via spinning bioluminescent wings. "It's the ugly duckling that turns into the swan," said Page. "This was another creature where I thought, 'Huh? This makes no sense to me.' And in the end, it looked really beautiful."

"We saw the fan lizard as a metaphor for the world of Pandora, and, in some ways, the movie," said Jon Landau. "When you first see it, it is an ugly toadlike creature. Then night begins to fall, and the fan lizard unfurls its wings, and its glowing disc-shaped wings light up the night sky in a magical beauty."

LEONOPTERYX

On the evolution of the leonopteryx design, lead creature designer Neville Page says, "The leonopteryx is the 'coveted' creature of the film; it's the one that chooses Jake, and Jake chooses it. Jim had a very specific vision of what he wanted it to be. Wayne Barlowe had done an early image, which really set the tone; I began there and evolved the look with Jim."

OPPOSITE, TOP: The first full realization of the leonopteryx by Barlowe. Conforming to the director's need for an X-form when the animal descended, it possessed a strong, distinctive head silhouette as well as the requisite four voluminous wings. Barlowe added thoracic nostrils to follow the biological consistency of Pandora.

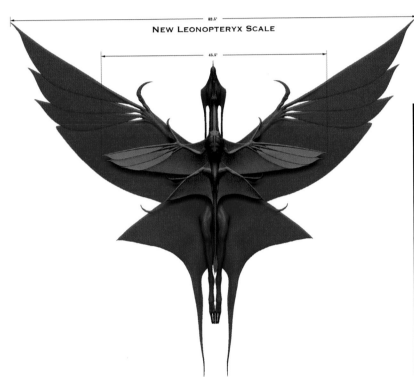

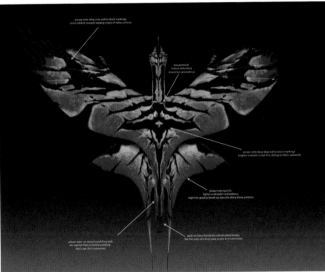

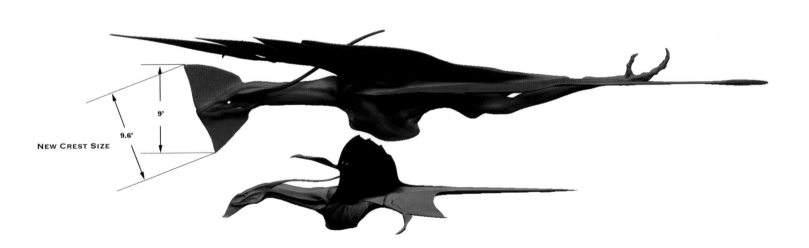

ABOVE, TOP LEFT and **ABOVE, BOTTOM:** Three-dimensional scale studies comparing the banshee to the leonopteryx, by Page.

ABOVE, TOP RIGHT and **OPPOSITE, BOTTOM:** Texture designs by Bartoli, based on direction from Cameron.

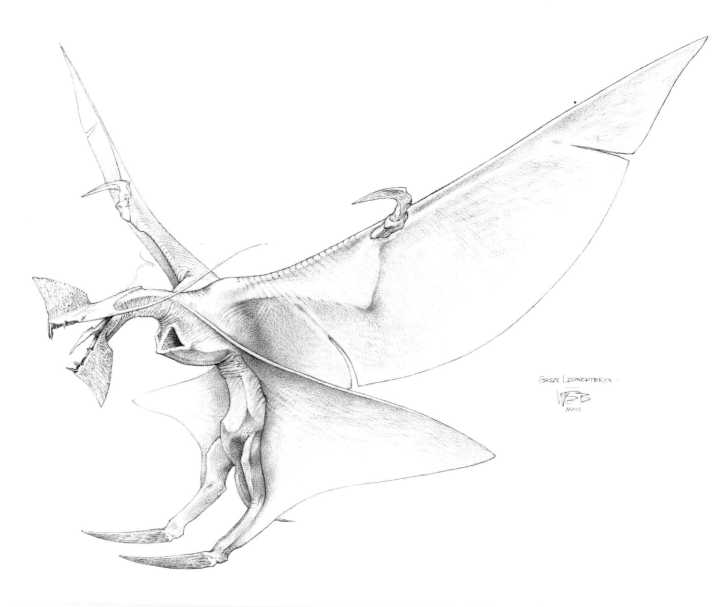

GREAT LEONOPTERYX

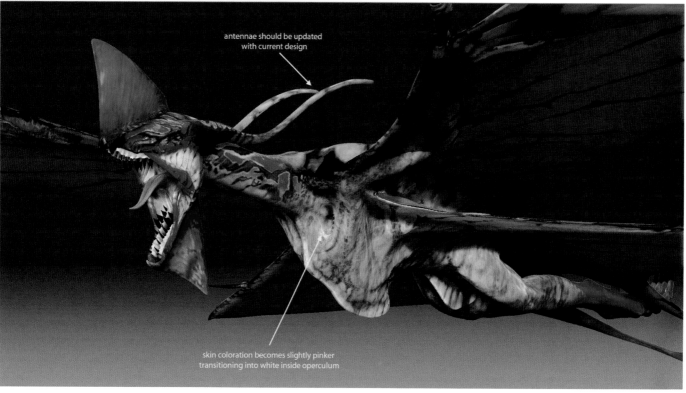

antennae should be updated
with current design

skin coloration becomes slightly pinker
transitioning into white inside operculum

BANSHEE

The banshees are among the most important creatures in the film, serving as Na'vi hunting mounts and playing a crucial role in the film's final battle. Of all the *Avatar* creatures, the banshee was the most difficult and time-consuming to design.

BELOW, TOP LEFT: Notes from Cameron to Page on the evolving banshee facial construction, including an exploration of the mechanics of its opening and closing jaws.

BELOW, TOP RIGHT: Final, approved 3-D model of banshee head and mouth design with texture overlay in Photoshop.

BELOW, BOTTOM: Concept illustrator Daphne Yap created many of the final design patterns for the banshee and leonopteryx for *Avatar*. Here is an example of one of the many detailed patterns employed over the course of the film.

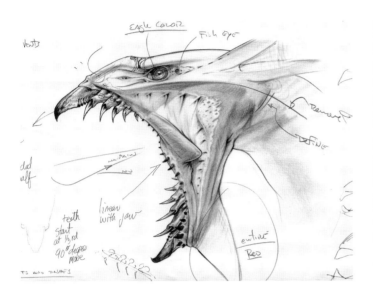

ABOVE: Early painting by concept artist Ryan Church. Often asked to "fill in gaps" in the visualization process, Church pulled together script excerpts, Page's clay sculpt (work-in-progress), and Barlowe's working color scheme. Page was exploring how the banshee walked on land; this image offered a view into a script moment with Jake as well as into the exploration of how the banshee's folded-up wings and folded-down claws would appear in a scene.

RIGHT: Neville Page works on banshee designs.

VIPERWOLF

BELOW, TOP LEFT: Early pencil sketch concept designs by Stan Winston Studio concept artist Jerad Marantz.

BELOW, TOP RIGHT: Cameron reviews viperwolf designs with the SWS team (John Rosengrant is at Cameron's left shoulder, key character designer Scott Patton is in the foreground, and Christopher Swift is to Rosengrant's left in the background).

BELOW, BOTTOM: Definitive black-and-white sketch of the viperwolf by Cameron.

OPPOSITE, TOP: These small, ballpoint notebook studies by Barlowe were his efforts not only to define the kinds of forms but also to convey the litheness and sinuous movement that the creature might display.

OPPOSITE, CENTER: This image by Page is a rough exploration of the six-legged Pandoran anatomy.

OPPOSITE, BOTTOM: This image by Stan Winston Studio is the final look as it was transmitted to Weta; note the glossy, metallic-plate appearance of the dark skin.

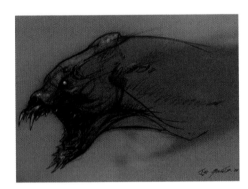

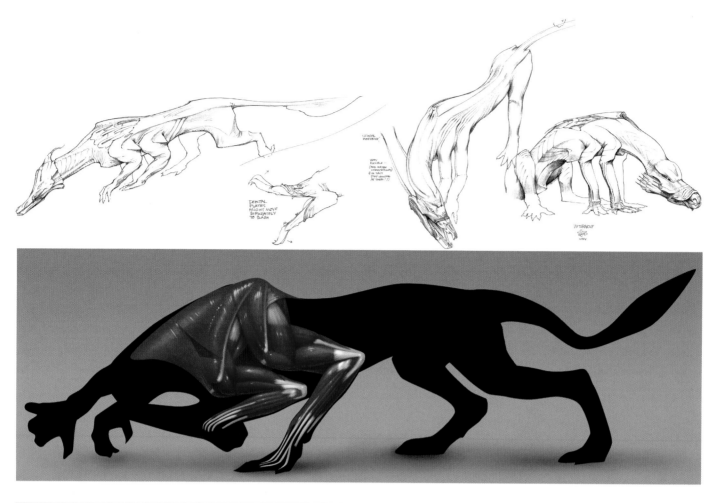

THANATOR

BELOW, TOP: A typical page of Barlowe pen sketches; in this case, studies addressing both the thanator's menacing silhouette and the location and action of its stabbing appendage. Like many sketches found on these pages, these images for the thanator depict a vast array of possible directions for its appearance.

BELOW, BOTTOM: In this frame grab from the movie, the thanator, ridden by Neytiri, snarls at Quaritch during their climactic battle. Note the "threat display" of its articulating armor plates and sensory whips, as described in the notes on Cameron's sketch (**OPPOSITE**).

OPPOSITE, TOP and **OPPOSITE, BOTTOM LEFT:** Thanator sketches and notes by Cameron. The director's sketches were used by Page in creating the final concept rendering of the thanator (**OPPOSITE, BOTTOM RIGHT**). These combined files were shipped off to Weta Digital as a blueprint for creating the final CG model of the creature.

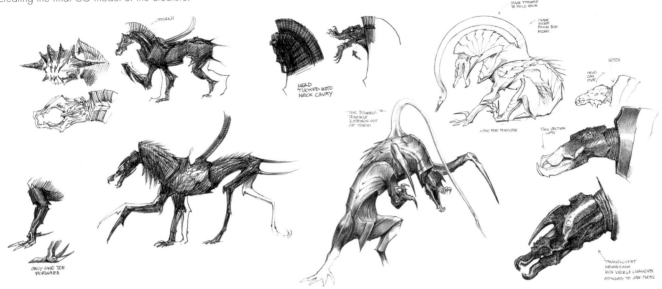

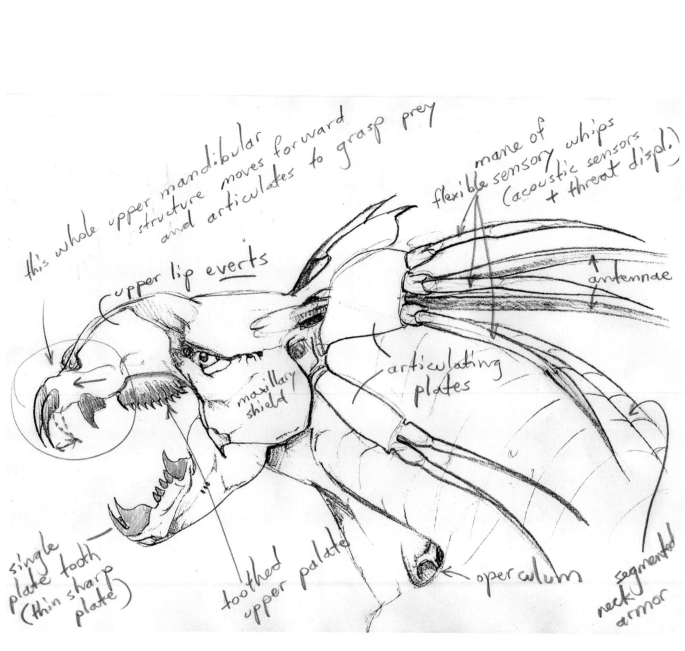

this whole upper mandibular structure moves forward and articulates to grasp prey

mane of flexible sensory whips (acoustic sensors + threat displ.)

upper lip everts

antennae

maxillary shield

articulating plates

single plate tooth (thin sharp plate)

toothed upper palate

operculum

segmented neck armor

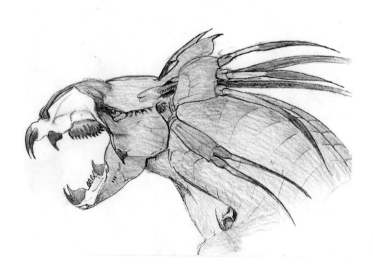

DIREHORSE

BELOW, TOP LEFT: These drawings by Barlowe are very early ballpoint studies. Says Page of the sketch at far right: "This design, this silhouette of the direhorse, is Barlowe's more than most. He came up with the feel for this kind of horny mane, and it stuck. We came in and started to define the textures. Then another person came in and interpreted it in clay—still one of my favorite sculpts—Stan Winston did a color pass, and then Weta got involved, who worked their magic."

BELOW, TOP RIGHT: Immediately following this approved center sketch by Barlowe was this image, in which the creature was filled out, color was added, and it was placed in an environment.

BELOW, BOTTOM: The direhorse was sculpted in chavent med clay; a photograph (**BOTTOM LEFT**) of this final sculpt was then imported into Photoshop. Textures, colors, and final details were added in and then merged with the background plate (**BOTTOM RIGHT**). Original sculpt and final image both by Winston Studio.

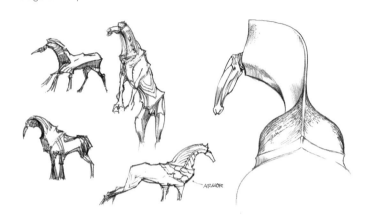

WOOD SPRITE

BELOW, BOTTOM LEFT: An early iteration of the mystical, floating "willathewisp" (the wood sprite's initial name) rendered in pencil. In this version it is clearly a botanic organism. Barlowe conceived of it steering by means of twin rows of iridescent cilia.

BELOW, TOP: More ornate variations by Page.

BELOW, BOTTOM RIGHT: The final design by Page.

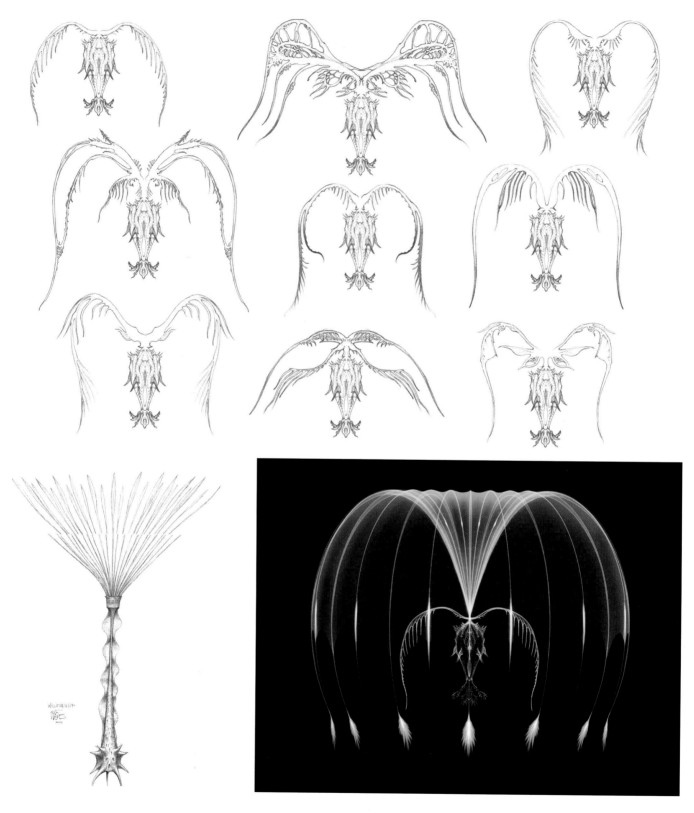

PROJECT 880- STURMBEEST
| REF# ART01 | DELIVERED to WETA: 10/26/06 |
| CAT: ART | ARTIST: YURI BARTOLI |

ABOVE: A Pandoran forest dweller, the sturmbeest, designed by Yuri Bartoli, travel in herds like buffalo; the Na'vi hunt them for meat. On the process of creature development for *Avatar*, Bartoli says, "Following Jim's guidance, we would begin with rough sketches; once this design was approved we would explore color and markings in Photoshop. The next step was to sculpt the creature in ZBrush, creating a digital maquette to refine the design from all angles and make sure the markings would 'read' in perspective. Working with Jim was always a very collaborative process, with a lot of discussion as to how the design of these creatures could further serve the story."

RIGHT: The mechanics of the tough, complex shell structure that makes the hammerhead so formidable are explored in this sculpture.

HEXAPEDE

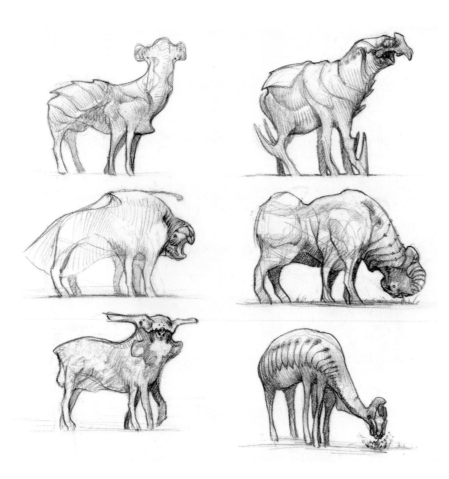

LEFT: Many different approaches to the hexapede were sketched, always attempting to ground the fantastic creatures in an understanding of real-world biology, as mandated by Cameron.

BELOW: A detail of the hexapede's digital maquette head. This approach—applied across the board—served several functions: It allowed the artist to resolve the design from all angles (as well as its color and markings in ways a flat painting could not) and allowed refinements to the designs by Cameron with the artist, preceding delivery to Weta for animation and lighting.

BOTTOM: An important part of the design process was understanding how the creatures would look in their environments on Pandora. All hexapede designs by Bartoli, including this final, approved version of the creature's look.

ABOVE, TOP: Early sketches by Page.

ABOVE, BOTTOM LEFT: Sketch by Barlowe; a Neytiri headdress study reflecting his interest in ancient cultures and working to convey a sense of a primitive culture utilizing nature-based aesthetics—skulls, nuts, or claws, for example—in ways similar to the Sumerians and Egyptians.

ABOVE, BOTTOM RIGHT: Barlowe at the art department.

"The theme of opening the eyes, or 'seeing,' runs throughout *Avatar*," noted Cameron. "The film was designed as a journey of perception, as much as a physical journey in an exotic world. A fundamental idea of the film is that it is necessary to look past cultural differences, past form or skin color, to see the truth of other people, to understand them for who and what they are."

The most important designs in the film would be the Na'vi themselves. Though artists at Stan Winston Studio would render very detailed and specific Na'vi and avatar designs much later—after actors had been cast in the roles—the original four artists generated rough Na'vi concepts based on Cameron's descriptions in the treatment. Initial Na'vi designs ran the gamut from a one-eyed, cyclops version to more anthropomorphic looks. After exploring the wilder ideas, artists spiraled back in to more human designs. For the story's central love story to work,

it was especially critical that Neytiri—whom Cameron had described in his treatment as "devastatingly beautiful, for a girl with a tail"—look appealing. Gills and antennae tended to work against that.

The team looked for ways to create "alienness" that wouldn't be off-putting. Animal features, such as catlike ears and a leonine nose, worked well, because they were inhuman but could express familiar emotional states, on the principle that a human audience knows the expressions of animals so well. The large, golden eyes, four times the size of a human eye by volume, also deviated from a human look, but without being ugly—in fact, quite the opposite, as they gave the Neytiri designs an otherworldly beauty.

Preliminary concepts illustrated the Na'vi as blue-skinned characters with—in addition to their articulated ears and catlike eyes and noses—long and lean bodies, and hands with only three fingers. Jordu Schell worked out the

Pencil studies by Barlowe. **ABOVE, LEFT:** Here, Barlowe explores Neytiri's grace and power (summer 2005); The more cursorial, elongated heels—for running—were to further distinguish Na'vi biology from human; **ABOVE, RIGHT:** This color treatment of the original pencil drawing reflected Cameron's desire for interesting stripes laid against a blue undertone.

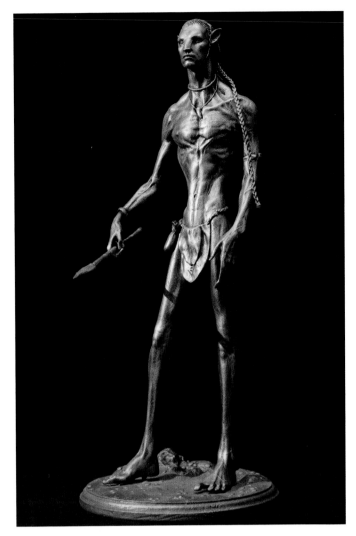

Finished bronze sculptures of Neytiri and Jake's avatar (**ABOVE**, **TOP LEFT** and **TOP RIGHT**) by Jordu Schell (**ABOVE**, **BOTTOM LEFT**). Throughout production, 3-D scans of these sculpts were used as "master reference."

RIGHT: John Rosengrant works with a Na'vi-size, ten-foot model of Jake's avatar (work-in-progress).

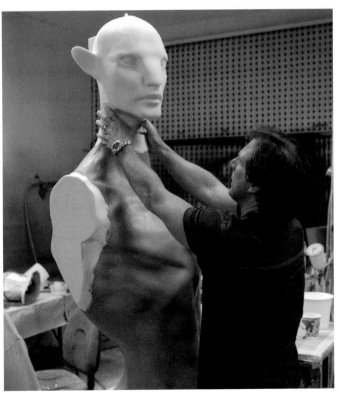

characters' bodily proportions and attributes on paper first and then in sculpted clay maquettes that suggested Na'vi attitude and bearing.

One of the defining drawings in discovering the design of the Na'vi was Cameron's own depiction of Neytiri, the Na'vi princess, which he presented to the concept art team. "That drawing is still my favorite piece of artwork that was done on the show," said Jordu Schell. "It was a very simple sketch. The edges of the head weren't even there. It was just her features sort of floating on a grayish-brown background. But it gave me a really good idea of what Jim was after."

The design team also created a range of looks for the avatars, which would have slightly more anthropomorphic features as a result of their controllers' DNA, but how heavily to weight them toward their human (versus Na'vi) side was a question without an answer for a long time. Artists rendered drawings of the characters with smaller, rounded ears, like those of a human, and then with more pointed, larger Na'vi ears. They drew avatars with Na'vi amber eyes pulled toward the side of the head, like an animal's, and then with downsized human eyes, positioned nearer the front.

In the end, the avatars would look very much like the Na'vi, but with skin that was a slightly lighter shade of blue and facial characteristics that subtly resembled the actors playing them. At this early stage of Na'vi and avatar design, of course, no one knew who those actors would be, but to get a general idea of how an actor's visage might shine through a Na'vi face, the designers referenced photographs of a variety of actors and models and incorporated their features with those of the Na'vi in sketches and paintings. At Cameron's direction, the artists avoided using photographs of well-known actors, as he didn't want to become accustomed to seeing Jake's avatar, for example, resembling a known star. "At one point," Yuri Bartoli recalled, "we were going to do a concept painting with an actor who was under consideration, but that got shot down, because Jim didn't want to get locked into an avatar that looked like that actor." Later in the process, Stan Winston Studio would develop Na'vi and avatar designs much more fully and, after actors were cast, incorporate specific actors' facial features into final designs.

The initial concept-development phase lasted for several months, and it was a period of tremendous creative energy and productivity. "I've worked with directors who don't have a clear idea of what they want," said Bartoli—

who would stay with the *Avatar* production from these early beginnings until its completion in 2009—"and because they don't have that clarity, they want designers to throw anything and everything at them. They want a huge volume of stuff that they can pick from, but that wastes a lot of good drawings and designs, and it takes up a lot of time. Jim, because of his background, had a very clear idea of what he wanted. He was still open to suggestions, but he was able to give us very clear direction."

"Working with Jim is nervewracking sometimes," added Jordu Schell, "because he is very specific about what he wants and he can be harsh with his opinion. But he also pushes you to do the best work of your career. I've worked for plenty of directors who just immediately say, 'Yeah, that's great,' and you mold it, and it's done. Whereas getting a little compliment from Jim would make your whole week! But when he tells you he likes something, you know it's true. And when you finally produce something that he likes, it is a tremendous feeling of accomplishment, because of his high standards. I don't think I've ever been held to standards as high as I was on this film."

As the concept artists worked at Cameron's Malibu house, *Avatar*'s technical development was unfolding on a stage twenty-five miles away in Playa Vista, with Rob Legato—a veteran visual-effects supervisor who had spearheaded *Titanic*'s Academy Award®–winning effects—overseeing the effort. Legato's involvement in *Avatar*, which would end after the development phase, had its origins in a phone call he had made to his friend Jim Cameron a few months before. In that call, Legato described a concept he had developed while working on CG shots for an airplane-crash sequence in Martin Scorsese's film about Howard Hughes, *The Aviator* (2004). As visual-effects supervisor for that film, Legato had been frustrated in his efforts to direct CG shots, due to the detached nature of the process. As always when dealing with the CG process, Legato first had to *describe* the camera work he wanted on a shot and then wait days or weeks to see the computer animation of what he had described. Often, that first attempt was not quite right, and Legato would describe the shot in more detail, then wait, again, for another iteration. That back-and-forth process could go on and on without the CG artist exactly nailing Legato's vision.

The core problem with the process was the inability of a director or visual-effects supervisor to "put his hands"

on the camera within the CG world. By describing camera movement, framing, and style, rather than being able to operate the camera, there was inevitably a gap between what the director had in mind and what wound up on-screen. "I'd look at a shot they'd created, and say, 'It's just not right,'" Legato recalled of *The Aviator* crash sequence. "'Yes, you put a 14-mm lens on it because I asked you to; but I *really* wanted you to put a 14-mm on it and move a little to the right.' It is all about a director's particular visual sense. Mine is different than Jim's; Jim's is different than Michael Bay's; Michael Bay's is different than Martin Scorsese's. Everybody has his own eye and sensibility, and to translate that through an intermediary—especially a CG person who has never been on the set with a camera—is very difficult. Something that you could do yourself on-stage in a second can wind up taking a very long time to translate to a CG artist."

Exasperated by the inefficiency of the process, Legato and his effects team rigged a system that would enable him to operate the camera within a CG scene, much like a gamer moves within a video-game environment using joystick controls. Instead of joysticks, however, Legato used camera pan-and-tilt wheels that were motion-captured in real time so that their movement could be instantly translated to movement within the CG scene. "What we were motion-capturing could have been anything I was moving around," Legato explained. "It could have been a rock or a stick. It didn't matter *what* the object was; all that mattered was that I was moving it *as if* it was a camera, and that it had markers on it so that it could be motion-captured. We just figured that rather than use a rock, we might as well motion-capture a camera, since that's what I was used to working with. So we rigged these pan-and-tilt wheels to accept live input." Makeshift as it was, the system allowed Legato to experiment with camera moves in CG shots; just as he would have done with a live-action camera, he executed many iterations of a shot very quickly—one with the camera move a little faster, another a little slower, one more to the right, another more to the left.

Working with Glenn Derry, his technical colleague on *The Aviator*, Legato had essentially created a "virtual camera"—a camera that could be motion-captured so that an operator could move it within a virtual, CG landscape in real time—and he recognized that Jim Cameron would be very interested in the idea. "Jim likes doing things himself," said Legato, "because he knows exactly what he

wants. He wants to control what the shot is, rather than have someone else show him what his shot is. So I called him up and told him what I did on *The Aviator*. Then, when it came time to do *Avatar*, he had the time, the money, and the wherewithal to take it to the next level, to amplify it so he could work in a very director-centric way."

With the virtual-camera concept, a big piece of the *Avatar* puzzle fell into place. But committing to this approach required a major decision on the part of the filmmakers. Cameron had originally planned to shoot background "plates" in real rain forest locations, to which he would add the CG characters and animals. But using the virtual camera to create shots meant that live-action background plates could *not* be used, because the movement of the camera would be determined at the virtual stage, not in the live-action plate.

The decision to make the film using a virtual production process meant that every leaf of every plant, every blade of grass, every bit of the Pandoran rain forest would have to be CG. Suddenly, the production faced a whole new world of challenges. "Creating photoreal CG environments, we knew, would be as big a task as creating the CG characters," Cameron remarked. "New tools for lighting and rendering would need to be created. And the design and execution of the CG 'assets,' all the plants trees, rocks, and skies of the world of Pandora, would need to be done at a higher level than had ever been done before. Gollum had worked—but how much of that was because the backgrounds had been photographed in the real world, and only the Gollum character was added with CG?" The team realized that the same uncompromising discipline that would go into making photo-real characters would now be needed for the environments. The movie would need CG characters in a CG world, and all done to a level of photo-reality that was unprecedented so that the CG scenes would cut in with the live-action scenes of actors on sets. "We all knew that we were holding hands and jumping off a cliff, at this point. There was no precedent for what we were about to do."

Real-time motion capture was the key to the virtual camera and the critical difference between what Cameron wanted to do on *Avatar* and what Robert Zemeckis had done on *The Polar Express*. On that and other performance-capture films, actors' performances on the motion-capture stage could not be seen as their CG characters until much later, after the initial performance capture had been cut and pasted

and thoroughly manipulated by computer animators. For *Avatar*, Cameron wanted to be able to see, *immediately*, how the captured performance translated to the CG character—or, at least, a crude version of the CG character—so that he could direct the actors accordingly. Tracking and streaming the movement of the actors on the stage and the movement of the camera, all in real time, would do just that.

The capacity to immediately see the actors' performances in their CG characters not only would be beneficial to Cameron as the director, but it also would be a tremendous boon to the actors. "On the playback monitors," said Glenn Derry, "the actors would be able to see and thus *feel* the difference between being human and being Na'vi. It would make them carry themselves a little differently. It wouldn't just be this abstracted process where everybody had to envision what their characters would look like later."

Through the virtual camera and real-time performance capture, Cameron would be able to direct all-CG shots—which would make up a large percentage of the shots in *Avatar*—just as he would live-action shots, with his CG characters and locations right there in his camera's eye. "Jim would be there," explained Derry, "framing up his shots, directing the talent with a camera in hand, looking at the virtual environment. He would be shooting live performances and getting real-time feedback during the shoot. Just like when shooting live action, he'd be able to see if he needed to put an actor up on an apple box to get a better eyeline, for example. You'd do that on a normal film—why not in this motion-capture world?"

"By allowing Jim to actually hold the 'camera' and work this way on *Avatar*," added Rob Legato, "it made for a very fluid, organic quality to creating CG shots. Jim

would still be out there with the camera, fishing around for a shot, just as he would on a live-action set."

In many respects, this virtual-production setup would be *better* than shooting live action. Cameron would be working with the actors on a stage that was empty of everything except simple forms to give them objects to walk around or climb over or duck under, so major set construction and dressing would not be necessary. There would be none of the crowd control or noise issues associated with location filming. There would be no lighting or camera setups to eat up time or distract the actors. At its essence, virtual production would simply be actors on a stage, performing emotionally driven scenes, guided by their director.

To determine the feasibility of virtual production, Cameron engaged Legato, Derry, and a team of technicians and CG artists to refine the makeshift virtual-camera system they had devised for *The Aviator*, using state-of-the-art, real-time motion-capture technology. Over the course of several weeks, the team conducted real-time tests with a motion-capture firm, while also exploring what form the virtual camera might take and how it would interface with the motion-capture computers. "We were just coming up with the basics of how one would approach filming this

movie on Pandora," Derry recalled. "At this stage, it was just, 'Hey, how are we going to do this?' None of the tools we ended up using were constructed yet."

The tech team also looked into the state of facial-capture technology. As impressed as Cameron had been with Gollum in the *Lord of the Rings* films, he knew that actor Andy Serkis's performance had served only as the *basis* of the CG character. Producing the compelling final performance had required a tremendous amount of keyframe animation for every Gollum shot. Essentially, animators had tracked the motion capture to the Gollum computer model, but had then gone in by hand, manipulating slider controls on the computer to create expressions by manually moving the character's facial muscles, eyes, and mouth.

But Cameron didn't want to leave his Na'vi and avatar performances so entirely to animators. Rather, he wanted to direct actors on the performance-capture stage and know that those *exact* performances would be translated, intact, to the CG characters. Cameron wanted to assure the actors that they weren't just doing voice work, and that every minute detail of their physical and emotional performance on the motion-capture stage would be retained in the final character.

Two main facial-capture methodologies were currently available, and the tech team did tests with both. One option was marker-based, with motion-capture cameras tracking markers on the face of the subject just as they would track Scotchlite markers on the body. The second option was an image-based approach that would employ standard cameras to record the facial performance. This image-based method would result in less data up front, and would thus require CG artists to build much more sophisticated computer facial models, capable of extrapolating a full performance from that lower-level data, but it would be more production-friendly overall.

The filmmakers opted for the second approach. To simplify the onstage setup, Cameron decided that he could capture the relevant facial information from a single camera mounted to a head rig and placed directly in front of the actor's face. Others argued that multiple cameras positioned around the actor's face would be necessary, but Cameron insisted that if the facial model of the CG char-

acter was rigged thoroughly enough, it could extrapolate and build a performance from the lesser information garnered by a single camera. Cameron and his actors would be able to work in a very large volume—large enough to capture horse runs and other big action pieces—and yet still have a highly intimate, close capture of the actors' faces. Glenn Derry agreed that the single-camera setup might suffice, and he and his team set about building a head rig. The rig consisted of a helmet with a miniature boom arm, similar to those on head mics worn by big-venue rock and pop performers. At the end of that boom sat a very small, standard-definition camera that would record the movement of the actor's face.

The building of hardware and refinement of software would continue for the next couple of years, but by the time Cameron had returned from a two-month diving expedition at the end of August 2005, the tech team had built a prototype virtual camera that resembled a typical motion-picture camera, with eyepiece and magazine,

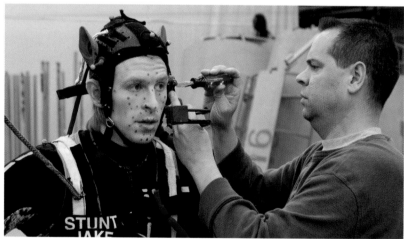

A key innovation enabling the film's production to create actor-driven, full-CG performances was the use of facial-capture technology. Employing image-based helmet camera rigs (built by Glenn Derry, including a miniature boom arm and custom-fit fiberglass helmets by SWS), these head rigs were worn by the actors throughout performance-capture production. Weta animation supervisor Andy Jones oversaw the CG artists' efforts to pull all the digital pieces together and bring precision to the end result.

OPPOSITE: Cameron demonstrates the second-generation molded head rig to visiting DreamWorks CEO Jeffrey Katzenberg at Playa Vista, late August 2007.

ABOVE, TOP: Zoë Saldana and Laz Alonso reviewing video, late May. **ABOVE, BOTTOM LEFT:** Sam Worthington's stunt double, Reuben Langdon, getting a minor head-rig adjustment, early May. **ABOVE, BOTTOM RIGHT:** Worthington, mid-April, all at the performance-capture stage at Playa Vista in 2007.

RIGHT: Cameron with the second-generation camera, the ring cam, mid-February 2007. Here, Cameron is showing the camera to his friend, Jimmy Iovine, head of Interscope Records.

ABOVE: A month and a half later, the production had graduated to the third-generation swing cam (April).

OPPOSITE: Peter Jackson, Richie Baneham, Steven Spielberg, Glenn Derry, and Cameron, Playa Vista, late November 2006.

presumably the general shape and form with which a film director would be most comfortable. The team also had set up a temporary pipeline that allowed them to stream live motion-capture data onto a digital character in real time. This beta virtual camera and real-time performance-capture pipeline so surpassed even the technically savvy Cameron's expectations, it took him most of a day to fully understand what the tech team had put together. By the end of that day, it was clear to Cameron that the system was sufficiently functional to allow him to shoot a prototype scene that would showcase the technology and prove the viability of virtual production.

Cameron chose the scene in which Jake meets Neytiri after she saves him from the pack of viperwolves as his prototype. The scene, at that point, was still in treatment form, so Cameron fleshed it out with dialogue and expanded it to five screenplay pages. Since it was too early to cast the real actors for the movie, Cameron found two actors to temporarily play the leads (still named "Josh" and "Zuleika" at this point) expressly for the prototype.

Yunjin Kim, who would later become well known on television's *Lost,* and Daniel Bess were set to play the leads only a day or so before the test shoot. Kim and Bess were suited up in motion-capture suits and head rigs, and shot on the performance-capture stage. "They both embraced the new technology," Cameron recalled, "and threw themselves into the roles, even though most of the technical details of the shooting had not been worked out. If they were skeptical about this crazy new way of making a film, they didn't show it, but rather took the assignment very seriously."

Live performance-capture data was fed into the pipeline software, resulting in an instant, real-time visualization of the digital characters the actors were portraying, interacting within a digital environment. "We had built all the digital environments we needed for this prototype scene," said Nolan Murtha, an early member of the tech crew, who would serve as digital-effects supervisor for virtual production. "We built the bridge where Neytiri and Jake meet. We built the waterfall in the background and the big purple fluorescent upside-down mushroom plants. All of those elements were there for the prototype." The environmental elements were very crude, however, and would only evolve into their final forms over the course of the next four years.

Kim's and Bess's body movements were captured by the motion-capture system, and their facial performances were recorded using the head-rig cameras. High-definition (HD) cameras, handheld by operators working within the motion-capture Volume provided reference images that would be used later by the animators for matching actors' facial expressions.

Cameron and Landau sent all of the motion capture, HD, head-rig, and locked-off video reference to Industrial Light & Magic, the company charged with creating the final rendered scene with computer-generated environments and a computer-generated "Josh" and "Zuleika."

Under the supervision of visual-effects supervisor Dennis Muren—a multiple Academy Award® winner who had worked with Cameron on some of his most groundbreaking films—ILM took the capture data and transformed it into a fully rendered forty-second scene, which was then delivered back to Lightstorm Entertainment, Cameron's Santa Monica production company. "To save time," Nolan Murtha noted, "ILM only finished a short section of the scene. Getting half a minute out in a few weeks was taxing enough, considering it would take us three years to do the other two hundred minutes of the movie!" To help refine the prototype animation, Cameron and Landau hired animation director Richard Baneham, who had been one of the animators responsible for the Gollum performance in the *Lord of the Rings* films. "Richie" Baneham would prove himself, over the next three years, to be an absolutely critical member of the team, eventually taking on second-unit directing duties and acting as Cameron's creative "right hand" in bringing the characters to life.

Cameron and Landau presented the finished prototype to Twentieth Century Fox in a split-screen setup, with half of the screen running reference images of the original actor performances from the motion capture stage and the other half showing the corresponding performance of the CG characters. The prototype was proof of concept that an emotional performance could be extracted from an actor and used to create a sustained performance in a CG character. Just as importantly, the reams of concept art suggested that *Avatar* would introduce audiences to an utterly original, fantastic world in a way not achieved since George Lucas's *Star Wars* (1977).

Still skeptical about the project, Fox reluctantly agreed to move forward with *Avatar*. "At the end of the presentation," recalled Jon Landau, "Fox felt that the characters could be compelling enough to watch for an entire film. Delivering this prototype was only one of a number

of things we needed to present before moving forward. Two very critical things were still outstanding—a script and a budget."

Even if the film could be done (and the prototype went a long way, but not all the way to showing that it could), there was still the question of whether an audience would go with it. The Fox executives were still skeptical that blue alien characters could carry a movie. They were dubious about the tails, in particular. And they were concerned that the prototype did not demonstrate the final level of "photoreality" that could be accomplished only through the economies of scale created by doing the entire project.

Fox's anxiety about *Avatar* was expressed at the end of the meeting, when one of the executives shook his head and said to Landau and Cameron, "I don't know if we're crazier for letting you do this, or if you're crazier for thinking you *can* do this. . . ."

OPPOSITE and **BELOW**: Final shots from the forty-second ILM "prototype" (created under the supervision of Academy-Award®-winning visual effects veteran Dennis Muren) showing versions of Neytiri and Jake based on Yunjin Kim (known for her work on the television program *Lost*) and Daniel Bess (*24*, *Grey's Anatomy*). Presented to FOX by Cameron and Landau as a "proof of concept" of the potential for performance-capture technology, the fully rendered scene demonstrated the technical viability of infusing an emotional, actor-driven performance into a fully computer-generated character; the forest background is 100 percent computer generated, which also proved that approach to be viable. Animation director Richie Baneham—responsible for the famous Gollum soliloquy sequence from *The Lord of the Rings: The Two Towers* (2002)—was initially brought on to refine the prototype animation; he remained on the production for the next four years.

LEFT: Kim and Bess, under direction from Cameron, performing the prototype scene.

TWO

ÄIE: VISION

Still without an official green light from Fox, Cameron spent the first five months of 2006 writing the first full draft of the screenplay from his original treatment, cutting some of the dense backstory, much of which he'd included for his own clarification as he invented the world of Pandora and its people. After a first go-through, the screenplay was still an unworkable two hundred–plus pages long, so Cameron discarded more chunks of story in a second round of cuts, finally trimming the screenplay to 148 pages, the same length as his *Titanic* screenplay.

Cameron and Landau also accelerated the design effort, bringing on production designers Rick Carter and Robert Stromberg to oversee a much-expanded art department. The new team of artists, along with the original "Malibu Five," would continue design work in offices at Lightstorm Entertainment. The art department's task was to develop Pandora's lush jungle environments—all of its spectacular plant life, ground cover, mountains, and waterways—as well as the Hell's Gate military and science compound that serves as the RDA's home base on Pandora.

Prior to *Avatar*, Robert Stromberg had been credited on many high-profile film projects as a concept artist and matte painter. Acquainted with his work on *Solaris* (2002) and at the recommendation of co-producer Brooke Breton, Cameron brought Stromberg on to *Avatar* when he was preparing the

OPPOSITE: Worthington stands with a full-size model of a male Na'vi on set in New Zealand (mid-February 2008).

ABOVE, TOP: Cameron with production designer Rick Carter reviewing Samson designs at Weta Workshop in New Zealand, mid-February 2007.

ABOVE, BOTTOM In May, back at Playa Vista, Cameron on set with production designer Robert Stromberg. Stromberg and Carter went on to win an Academy Award® in art direction together for their work on Avatar.

OPPOSITE: One of the first paintings created depicting the landscape of Pandora, this image by Stromberg served as an essential reference painting for the Lightstorm Art Department for sometime thereafter.

prototype presentation for Fox. "I got a call to help Jim out for just a couple of weeks for this studio presentation," Stromberg recalled. "I'd never met him, and I had no idea what the project was. I asked the producers, and they couldn't tell me—but they did say that it was set on an alien planet with floating mountains and things like that. That's all I had! I was going to meet with Jim the next day, and I stayed up all night and did two images of what I felt this alien landscape could be. And then I went in and met Jim, and put that on the monitor, and he stood up, pointed at the screen, and said, 'That's the first time I've seen my planet!'" Stromberg would remain on the project well beyond the Fox presentation, and his contributions to the look of the film became so significant that Cameron and Landau, with Rick Carter's support, offered him a production-designer credit—Stromberg's first—and sealed the agreement with a handshake. He would later win the Oscar for *Avatar*'s production design, along with Rick Carter, the first time an Academy Award for production design was shared.

Rick Carter had many production-designer credits, having worked in that capacity on projects such as Steven Spielberg's *Jurassic Park* (1993) and Robert Zemeckis's *Forrest Gump* (1994) and *The Polar Express*. But Carter would later admit that nothing in his film experience had sufficiently prepared him for *Avatar*. When he first went into the Lightstorm offices to read the script, he found the world of Pandora as described in the screenplay so rich and abundant, so startling and fresh, that his attempt to visualize it made for very slow reading—more than three hours passed before he turned the final page.

What Carter picked up on immediately was the contrast between the Hell's Gate and Pandora forest environments, and how the reveal of that forest, as described in Cameron's screenplay, was reminiscent of the moment in *The Wizard of Oz* (1939) when Dorothy steps from her black-and-white Kansas farmhouse into the colorful land of Oz. Cameron, who had more than once cited *The Wizard of Oz* as his favorite movie, referenced that very moment in a line in the script, in which Colonel Quaritch, the commander of the RDA forces, tells the new recruits that they "are not in Kansas anymore."

The contrast between Pandora's natural forest and the Hell's Gate military-industrial complex would be reflected in the very different means by which the two environments would be created. Hell's Gate would consist primarily

of constructed physical sets, created with hammer, nails, paint, and putty. Pandora's jungle, however, would be realized entirely within the computer. "The main thing that was different conceptually in this film," noted Weta Digital visual-effects supervisor Joe Letteri, whose team of visual-effects artists would be responsible for creating that CG world, "was that so many of the sequences became *entirely* CG once you were in the jungle environment. We'd had a number of shots that were all CG on *Lord of the Rings*, and a bit more on *King Kong*, but for *Avatar*, once we left the human world and went into the jungle, we were pretty much in a CG environment the whole time."

To encourage very different aesthetics in the design of the two environments, the production designers agreed that Rick Carter would concentrate on designing Hell's Gate sets while Robert Stromberg focused on the organic world of Pandora's rain forest—what Cameron had described as "the Garden of Eden, with teeth and claws." "It brought two completely separate, contrasting statements to the story, visually," commented Stromberg, "which was great, because that is what's actually going on *in* the story. It was a fabulous collaboration."

Stromberg and his team designed Pandora environments for an entire year, first producing pencil sketches and then full-color paintings. "In some of the first [efforts]," recalled Stromberg, "we went really out there to see how far we could push it. And then, over time, we pulled back to something the audience could relate to,

something that equated, to some extent, to an Earth environment. You couldn't have an audience watch a film for two and a half hours, constantly trying to figure out what they were looking at. So we would often start with Earth environments, as fantastic as we could find but nevertheless something that registered with everyday things people see, and then we would take those Earth environments to an extreme, into an alien place."

Photography from the Guilin region of China, which features dramatic limestone formations, and from South American jungles provided valuable reference, but, although these natural settings and others served as a touchstone, Cameron encouraged the artists to create utterly original environments, to make Pandora a world unlike any seen before. "One of my pet peeves," commented Ryan Church, a concept artist who was hired by Rick Carter to join the Lightstorm art department, "is that in science-fiction movies we go to these other planets, but the planets are always 'the desert Southwest planet' or the 'glacier planet.' This was a *real* alien planet that Jim was designing; and the degree to which he thought through the ecosystems and the interactions—it was the first time I'd seen anything like that."

Artists took a "reverse powers of ten" approach to designing Pandora, starting with sweeping, big-picture views rendered in paintings, then narrowing those broad perspectives down to specific settings, and finally designing individual plants and trees. Key settings included the mystical Tree of Souls, the catalyst through which the Na'vi

connect to the spirits of their ancestors, and Hometree, the thousand-foot-tall tree that has housed Neytiri's Omaticaya clan for ten thousand years.

For the Tree of Souls, the designers again turned to the real world for inspiration, studying bonsai trees and replicating their twisted, knotted branches to depict an ancient look. For Hometree, form followed function. "Our first step with something like Hometree," said Ryan Church, "was to ask: How does this thing work? How do the Na'vi get in there? How do they bring their food in? How does this village sustain itself? We had to have all of those questions answered when they were put to us." Final Hometree–interior designs featured multiple levels of living spaces formed naturally within the massive hollow trunk, and augmented by the Omaticaya with their woven "tensile structures."

Cameron justified Pandora's oversize creatures and plant life by the low gravity levels on the moon. "The scale was just out of control," said concept designer Dylan Cole. "Even a standard tree was probably two to three hundred feet tall. The mountains were huge; the canyons were huge; the waterfalls were epic. Scale really enhanced the grandness and alienness of this planet."

After specific settings had been established, the artists concentrated on rendering individual plants, often scaling up small real-world succulents and exotic flowers to give them an otherworldly look. "We'd scale those up to ten, twenty, fifty times larger," said Cole. "Something that might be half an inch on Earth we'd blow up to a ten-foot-tall giant alien plant. We figured Earth is a better designer than we are. We couldn't design anything cooler than what already existed, and Jim felt that way, as well, and so we always tried to reference something real."

In one instance, that "something real" was a tree growing just a few minutes from the Lightstorm offices. "I was driving near the Santa Monica Pier one day," Robert Stromberg recalled, "and I saw this twisting pine tree in the park.

I thought it had a really cool look. So I took my camera to the park, lay down on my stomach, and took pictures of it, and from that, I created an image. When Jim saw it, he said, 'That's a shot in my movie.'" Marine life often served as reference for specific vegetation, as well. For example, the giant spiral-shaped plants that retract when Jake touches them were essentially large-scale versions of *Spirobranchus giganteus*, Christmas tree worms, a marine invertebrate.

Initially, artists illustrated the flora in shades of blue—as per Cameron's request—to tie it visually to the blue-fleshed Na'vi and distinguish it from Earth's green, but, eventually, they incorporated more greens to give audiences a familiar touchstone in the alien environment. Cyan-colored environments also would have made it difficult for CG artists to distinguish foregrounds from backgrounds, since they typically use blue-tinted atmospheric haze to create a sense of depth and distance.

OPPOSITE, TOP: Working to resolve the design of Hometree's interior, Steve Messing illustrated Neytiri walking along a massive helix; like a DNA strand, this helix twists around, providing a natural passageway for the Na'vi to move up and down the tree's central tiers. This concept later became part of the final design for the core of Hometree.

RIGHT: Frame grab depicting the grandeur of Pandora's daytime landscapes, including the enormous "Great Trees" that tower above the forests. Cameron sought a scientifically sound basis for every alien plant and creature on Pandora. The large scale of all of the moon's trees, for example, was due to Pandora's low gravity and the high density and carbon dioxide content of its atmosphere.

OPPOSITE, TOP: A study of the Hometree exterior by Messing. All of the foliage, moss, and vines were painted in layers so that Cameron could add or delete dressing as needed.

OPPOSITE, BOTTOM: An early depiction of Jake and Tsu'Tey fighting with staffs. In the final film, the two engage, instead, in a knife fight (Steven Messing).

BELOW: Jake joining the Na'vi nighttime gathering; painting by Messing.

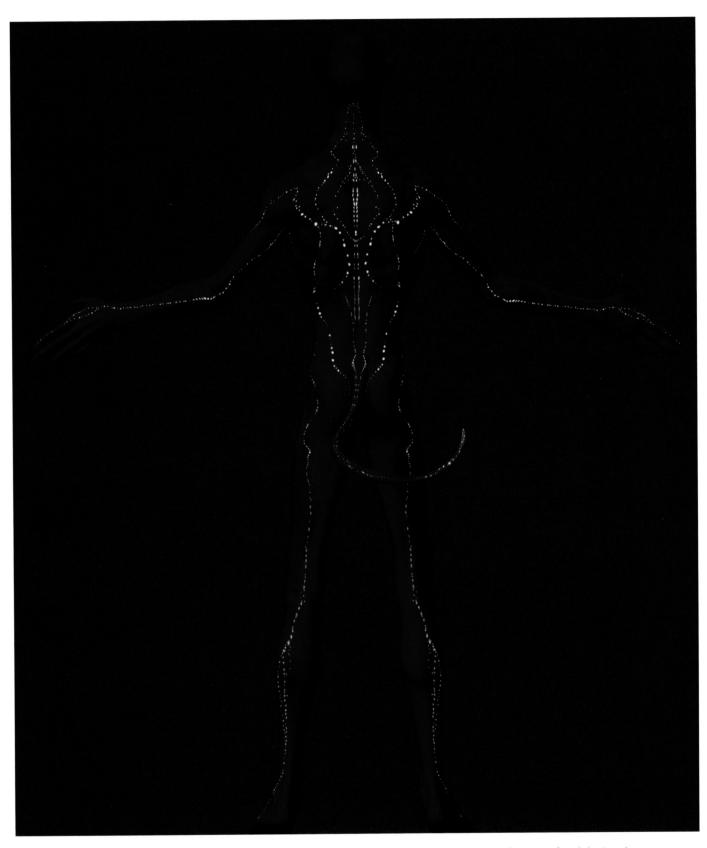

ABOVE: Stan Winston Studio spearheaded the creation of bioluminescent patterns and other markings for the Na'vi, working in Photoshop to produce many iterations from which Cameron could choose. Here, the final pattern for Jake's avatar's backside.

OPPOSITE, TOP: A study of the Tree of Souls by Stromberg.

OPPOSITE, BOTTOM: A "large-scale" view of the Tree of Souls by Stromberg.

OPPOSITE: A "hero angle" on the Tree of Souls, establishing the tree's final height atop the rock outcrop, as well as the tendril-like look of its branches, as opposed to more Earth-like willow branches and leaves of earlier paintings. Painting by Cole.

ABOVE, TOP: Quick sketch by Messing of Grace's death scene. Roots of the Tree of Souls form tendrils around her wounded body as Jake, Neytiri, Mo'at, and the clan ask Eywa to heal her. ABOVE, BOTTOM: Cameron working on set in New Zealand with actors Worthington and Sigourney Weaver in the Tree of Souls scene in which Grace is dying.

Bioluminescence was one of the most challenging creative aspects for the illustrators to realize. Displayed here is a small sampling of the hundreds of images explored—all spearheaded by Stromberg, per Cameron's direction—over the course of many months.

ABOVE: Early study by Cole illustrating Jake and Neytiri running through a network of bioluminescent moss. This moment was reinstated in the August 2010 theatrical re-release of the film.

RIGHT: Bioluminescent plantlife showing how light not only glows off the surface, but emanates from within (Stromberg).

OPPOSITE: Jake and Neytiri run across a network of tree branches in the bioluminescent jungle at night (Messing).

Bioluminescence was a ubiquitous feature of the jungle foliage, suggested by the original concept artists in neon colored-pencil drawings on black paper, a technique Cameron had used in designing the glowing aliens and their craft for *The Abyss*. Artists would continue to explore the look—and function—of the bioluminescence throughout the design stage and well into Weta Digital's final shot production. As Cameron saw it, the bioluminescence was the physical manifestation of the Gaia hypothesis, the idea that all of the ecological and physical components of a planet are interconnected. "Jim wanted the glow to visually suggest the actual links between roots and trees and everything else," said Ryan Church, "but in a subtle way, without hitting you over the head."

Creature designs, too, continued to evolve during this second year, with artists refining original black-and-white pencil sketches into full-color Photoshop renderings. Artists developed a bright color palette for the leonopteryx, for example, painting Photoshop patterns in iridescent shades of scarlet, gold, and midnight blue. "One of the things we wanted to do was introduce colors into creatures where you wouldn't normally see them," explained Jon Landau. "There are some incredible colors on creatures in our natural world, but they are generally on smaller creatures, whereas the large rhinoceroses and elephants are very gray. We wanted to introduce color into all of these characters."

"You're not going to find a large, predatory creature on [Earth] with bright, flashy colors," added Neville Page.

Jake and Neytiri touch heads together and breathe in each other's spirit, a traditional Maori greeting called the "hongi." Cameron borrowed this from Maori culture as an homage to New Zealand, where the film was shot (ABOVE). Early concept painting for the same scene by Messing (OPPOSITE).

"But we didn't care if a colorful predator was correct. It was more about creating something alien. Jim would often say, 'It's an alien planet, so anything goes.'" Daphne Yap, one of the new members of the expanded art department, created detailed and colorful markings for all of the creatures, a stage of the design process that came to be known as "Daphnization."

The artists also created bioluminescent patterns for many of the creatures, which—except for on the fan lizard and the Na'vi—went largely unseen. "We did a lot of nice bioluminescent designs for creatures that, unfortunately, we never see at night," said Yuri Bartoli, "so we never see the glowing pattern. Maybe for the sequel!"

After full-color Photoshop renderings were approved, artists sculpted creatures in clay to give Cameron a scaled model that he could touch and see in real-world lighting. Some moved into a 3-D sculpting program called ZBrush to create turntable computer models. Often, Cameron would sit with the artist at his workstation to suggest changes to the digital sculpt, which could be implemented on the spot, in real time. "Working digitally, you are able to do many different versions of something quickly," said Bartoli. "It was very interactive. Jim could sit there and drive the whole process."

The accelerated design effort also produced concepts for vehicles, aircraft, and other hardware, developed by lead vehicle designer TyRuben Ellingson, Ryan Church, and Ben Procter. Among the aircraft concepts were the Scorpion gunship, a twin-turbine rotorcraft equipped with four gimbal-mounted .50-caliber guns; the smaller Samson transport helicopter; and the Dragon assault gunship, deployed for combat missions. Spacecraft featured early in the film include the ISV Venture Star, which makes the five-year journey from Earth to Pandora, and the Valkyrie shuttle, which transports crews from the Venture Star to the moon's surface. The hardware designers also developed the Amplified Mobility Platform—the "AMP Suit"—an agile, powerful, weaponized hard suit worn by operators in the field to protect them from Pandora's hostiles and its toxic atmosphere.

Just as he had with the organic jungle designs, Cameron insisted that the military ships and hardware look fantastic but still reflect real-world science and technology. In every instance, artists had to be able to answer fundamental questions concerning why each piece of hardware would be built, and what its purpose would be. "Jim saw the AMP Suit, for example," said Jon Landau, "as the armor of the next century, so that infantrymen would no longer have to be put in harm's way of roadside bombs. Our artists fed off that idea."

LEONOPTERYX

25.14m span

BANSHEE

13.9m span

STINGBAT

4.27m span

TETRAPTERON

1.44m span

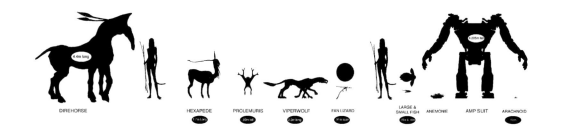

11m long

HAMMERHEAD

NAVI

6.4m long

STURMBEEST

5.75m long

THANATOR

4.4m long

DIREHORSE

HEXAPEDE

1.7m long

PROLEMURIS

.89m tall

VIPERWOLF

2.2m long

FAN LIZARD

.9m span

LARGE & SMALL FISH

.65m & .4m

ANEMONIE

AMP SUIT

4.205m tall

ARACHNOID

.15cm

SCORPION

SAMSON

DRAGON

BULLDOZER

GLOWING PURPLE WORM

Scale Comparisons: Meters
Drawn By: Neville Page
3-27-09
Rev: 10

THIS SPREAD: In the process of developing a three-dimensional, virtual world full of all manner of alien creatures and futuristic machines, scale and correct proportion were crucial elements for every aspect of production. Displayed here are the all size relationships displayed on the film's scale chart.

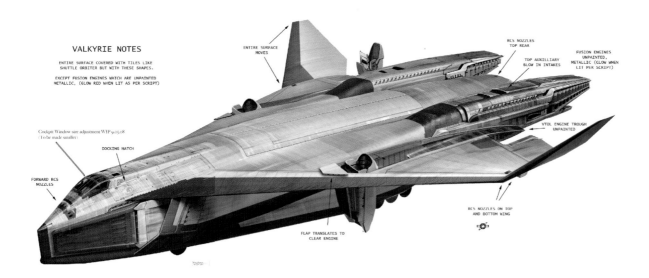

VALKYRIE NOTES

ENTIRE SURFACE COVERED WITH TILES LIKE
SHUTTLE ORBITER BUT WITH THESE SHAPES.

EXCEPT FUSION ENGINES WHICH ARE UNPAINTED
METALLIC, (GLOW RED WHEN LIT AS PER SCRIPT)

ENTIRE SURFACE
MOVES

RCS NOZZLES
TOP REAR

TOP AUXILLIARY
BLOW IN INTAKES

FUSION ENGINES
UNPAINTED,
METALLIC (GLOW WHEN
LIT PER SCRIPT)

VTOL ENGINE TROUGH
UNPAINTED

Cockpit Window size adjustment WIP 9.05.08
(To be made smaller)

DOCKING HATCH

FORWARD RCS
NOZZLES

RCS NOZZLES ON TOP
AND BOTTOM WING

FLAP TRANSLATES TO
CLEAR ENGINE

Concept illustrator Ryan Church's signature contribution was the Valkyrie shuttle, a transport vehicle largely designed to carry cargo (unobtainium) and passengers between Hell's Gate and the orbiting Venture Star. The Valkyrie, however, can also be pressed into service as a killing machine. Church conducted extensive aerodynamic research from previously classified NASA and DARPA technical papers, but his design also contains many elements reminiscent of Vietnam War era aircraft, such as the F-4 Phantom and the C-130 Hercules Transport. The story calls for the Valkyrie to drop two "daisy cutters" on the Tree of Souls, real explosives so named during the war because their impact (when tossed midflight out of Hercules's cargo ramps) would leave distinctive, daisy-shaped craters dotted across the southeast Asian landscape. Jake thwarts the effort to annihilate the Na'vi's most sacred site; his grenades land in the engine intake after the explosives had been armed, causing the Valkyrie to go into an uncontrolled roll and crash in a massive fireball. Church designed and built models of the cockpit, aft cockpit, cargo bay, and exterior for the Virtual Art Department; his specs (**ABOVE, TOP**) also went to SWS who fully fabricated the shuttle's cockpit.

ABOVE, BOTTOM: In this frame grab, the Valkyrie shuttle brings Jake and other recruits to Hell's Gate from the Venture Star.

ISV VENTURE STAR

The ISV Venture Star, though a fantasy vehicle, is based on sound principles of physics. The central five-hundred-meter truss, which elongates the Interstellar Vehicle (ISV), as noted in Ben Procter's final diagram (**BELOW, BOTTOM**), is designed to separate the crew section from the radiation generated by its antimatter drive. As seen in the film, the enormous twin antimatter engines are still glowing with heat from slowing the ship into the Alpha Centauri star system. The stack of large, flat shields protect the ship from space debris at relativistic speeds. Two Valkyrie shuttles are mated to the exterior via docking nodes for the six-year outbound journey. They will remain on Pandora as the ISV transports its cargo of unobtainium back to an energy-starved Earth. All other Venture Star designs on this page are by Procter, with additional design and modeling by Tex Kadonaga, Joe Hiura, and Rob Johnson.

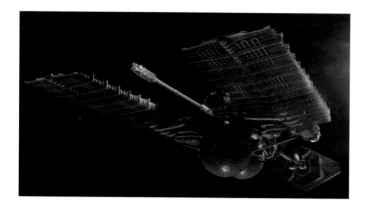 

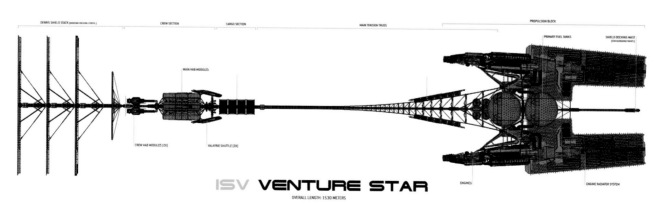

ISV **VENTURE STAR**

OVERALL LENGTH: 1530 METERS

ABOVE, TOP: Behind-the-scenes still of Stephen Lang on set in New Zealand in the Dragon cockpit set, mid-January 2008. ABOVE, BOTTOM LEFT: Among other things, vehicle designer TyRuben Ellingson was responsible for the AMP Suit, the Samson, the Scorpion gunship, the RDA bulldozers, and most of the Dragon design. ABOVE, BOTTOM RIGHT: This study model of the Dragon was assembled out of 3-D printed components by Weta Workshop in May 2007. OPPOSITE: Conceptual art of the final battle by Messing.

Artists applied the same real-world principles to aircraft, reasoning that a feature such as supersonic speed, which makes for cool-looking streaking effects shots, was both impractical and unnecessary for aircraft whose main function was to transport troops and hardware into the heart of a dense jungle. "We decided to come up with aircraft that could do vertical takeoffs and landings," said Landau, "because there were no landing strips on these planets. You just have to find a patch of land that you can land on."

Like all of *Avatar*'s designs, the final aircraft and hardware concepts were the product of meticulous attention to detail. "I remember showing Jim the Valkyrie shuttle," recalled Ryan Church, "and we went back and forth with that many times until it was a very realistic concept. It

wasn't like it is in a lot of movies, where a spaceship is just a cool-looking thing that glows at one end. It was really well thought-out. This was a director who wanted to know what kinds of bolts were holding the fusion engines on! I loved the fact that I got to step up to that level of detail."

Before they were through, the members of *Avatar*'s art department would produce many hundreds of drawings and sculpts of ships, tanks, AMP Suits, cranes, and aircraft—an impressive array of designs that Cameron would describe as the best he's ever had on a film. It was high praise, especially considering the fantastic hunter-killer aircraft and the endoskeletons from his *Terminator* films (1984 and 1991) the powerloaders from *Aliens* (1986), and other heavy-metal icons from Cameron's previous movies.

ABOVE, TOP LEFT: A five-foot-long model of the Samson produced by Weta Workshop showing what would ultimately be built as a full-scale mockup; it was created to study camera angles and techniques for live-action photography. **ABOVE, TOP RIGHT**: Study model of the Scorpion gunship tiltrotor by Weta Workshop.

OPPOSITE: Frame grab of Trudy's Samson diving into a gorge, as she gives the newbies a thrill ride. **FOLLOWING SPREAD**: Dr. Grace Augustine guides new avatars Jake and Norm on their first "sortie" into the Pandoran forest. Landing in a clearing, they set out on foot.

EARTH & HELL'S GATE

A resource-depleted Earth, originally considered for the film's opening, is a war-weary, over-populated place where cities have become corporate-dominated megalopolises and the air is not fit to breathe.

ABOVE: Jake's home city is depicted here by Cole—a bowl-shaped urban center with a garish, treelike advertising column as its central pillar. "It's a deliberate contrast to Hometree; where the Na'vi worship life and nature, humans worship technology, advertising, and industry," says Cole. RDA's interests are extended via the Venture Star to the naturally abundant, undisturbed alien locales of Pandora; its corporate footprint takes the shape of a pentagon in this aerial-view Photoshop painting of Hell's Gate by concept illustrator James Clyne (**OPPOSITE, RIGHT**).

OPPOSITE, LEFT: Hell's Gate development art by Clyne. For the perimeter, Clyne's research included studying industrial settings in Japan as well as the perimeter fences of the Gaza Strip and the U.S./Mexican border.

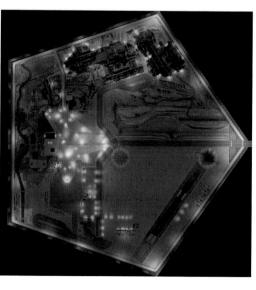

OPS CENTER

Concrete, steel, heavily worn, weathered surfaces, military culture, corporate hierarchy—these are some of the terms used to describe this "nerve center of Hell's Gate" to its first illustrators; a not-so-futuristic-looking, heavily fortified bunker out of which Selfridge runs the ever-expanding RDA corporate operations: an interstellar mining refinery, a Bio Lab and the avatar program, a flight tower and a private militia that is constantly out on patrol. Like a medieval fortress, this heavily armed outpost is designed to keep wildlife out and bring energy resources in; its singular strategic purpose is to expand the acquisition of Pandora's chief resource—the superconductive "unobtainium," an ore so powerful mountains float and rock formations curve into massive natural arches around it. Final 3-D models plus 2-D illustrations were supplied to Weta Digital.

ABOVE: Ops Center final 3-D model (shipped to Weta Digital for the next phase of design and production) by Victor Martinez, based upon art direction and designs by Procter and Clyne.

RIGHT: Valkyrie Shuttle designer and *Avatar* concept illustrator Ryan Church.

OPPOSITE, TOP and **OPPOSITE, BOTTOM**: Two angles from the finished film of the Valkyrie Shuttle coming in for a landing at Hell's Gate.

The art-department crews were not the only members of the *Avatar* team engaged in furious activity throughout that year. Simultaneously, the tech team was busy with what Glenn Derry called "toy making," writing the software and building the hardware that would make virtual production possible. "We were writing code and figuring out how we were going to make the virtual camera better," said Derry, "based on things we'd learned from the prototype."

Back in 2005, for the prototype test, Derry and his crew had built a virtual camera that resembled a typical motion-picture camera, reasoning that it would feel like a familiar object in Cameron's hands. Subsequent to the prototype shoot, the team built versions that looked less like a motion-picture camera, since all that was really needed in this "camera" was a small monitor that would enable Cameron to see his digital characters in a digital environment, plus software that would tie the camera to the performance-capture system so that camera movement could be captured and displayed on the monitor in real time.

For the new version of the virtual camera, Derry mounted the monitor to a swing mechanism; as a result, no matter how the camera was positioned—upside down, right side up, or sideways—the monitor would always be facing Cameron, enabling him to see his CG scene. Derry dubbed this version, which weighed seven pounds and could be easily handheld, the "swing" cam, and it became the camera Cameron used most often throughout production, even after the tech crew had produced versions weighing only two pounds. "You can hand a fiddle player a Stradivarius," commented Derry, "but he's likely to just look at it, and say, 'This is great, thanks, but I'm sticking with my fiddle.' Jim got used to the feel of that first swing cam, and that's the one he wanted to use throughout."

The swing cam and its successors also had push-button controls that essentially gave Cameron access to an entire camera department. He could change scales or execute aerial, dolly, and crane moves, all at the touch of a button. "Basically," said Jon Landau, "every single piece of equipment you see on a live-action set, we could replicate with this virtual camera. We could say, 'Make me a Steadicam,' and the computer would make the virtual camera a Steadicam. We could say, 'I want a crane move. Let's start at one hundred feet, and when the actor says his line, I want to be in a close-up.' And the computer could build that curve."

Meanwhile, Tim Bicio, another member of the tech crew, was busy creating the production's "Gaia" system.

"This was the hub of all things digital," said Landau, "a custom-built digital-asset-management system that would contain all of the artwork, track all of the performance-capture takes, be the repository for all of the visual-effects work, and more."

Technical crews also moved forward with assembling the performance-capture setup, collaborating with Giant Studios, the company that would provide all of the motion-capture services for the film. Giant Studios had won the assignment largely due to its system's advanced biomechanical-solving properties, which meant that if an area of a performer's body was obstructed from the motion-capture cameras mounted in the ceiling, the system could fill in the obstructed area on the skeletal figure in the computer. That ability would be crucial to *Avatar*'s production, since the motion-capture stage would be littered with set pieces and operators holding HD reference cameras, all of which would block actors from the cameras at one point or another.

Giant's superior biomechanical-solving properties also would allow for better real-time performance capture, since artists wouldn't have to go in and fix obstructed areas by hand. "What is unique about our system," said Giant Studios performance-capture supervisor Matt Madden, "is that we're able to do five, six, seven characters in real time, all at once, with moving props and everything. [With *Avatar*, we] could get all of that motion live, which had never been done before, especially in production conditions."

Purely by coincidence, Giant Studios was, at the time, located at Playa Vista, in a building next door to the one in which most of the *Avatar* shoot would take place. As Giant started building the performance-capture setup on one stage, they were therefore able to easily test the workflow for virtual production in the adjacent facility. "The fact that Giant was next door was really advantageous," noted Glenn Derry. "A lot of how this movie got made, at least from a technical standpoint, had to do with the fact that the teams were so willing to work with one another. Everybody was just there to figure it out. It was very collaborative, which was unique to anything I've ever done in this business."

Avatar's Playa Vista set was a dusty, old warehouse with a paper sign that read "Project 880"—the name used to preserve the secrecy of the endeavor—plastered on the door. Inside there were no props, no sets being built, no

Integral to *Avatar*'s production was the virtual camera, which was not really a camera at all, but a small video monitor with handles. Tracked by the motion-capture system, it showed the director a real-time image of the virtual world, including actors' performances that were captured days or even months earlier. As Cameron operated the camera within these pre-recorded scenes, new "camera moves" were recorded, which then became the actual moves used for the final shots. Cameron worked in the empty Volume for over a year after he was finished with the actors, operating the CG camera moves for the movie. Legato describes the process this way: "If he can shoot it just the way he would shoot it if a ten-foot-tall blue alien were there for real, then there's a live, organic quality that you get. It's not intellectually wrought, it's viscerally wrought" (*The Futurist*, p. 238). Though lighter-weight versions were later built, Cameron preferred the seven-pound "swing cam"—so named due to a swing mechanism that kept the monitor facing him, no matter how he positioned the camera—and used it throughout production.

ABOVE, TOP LEFT and **ABOVE, TOP CENTER**: Side and direct views of the swing cam.

ABOVE, TOP RIGHT: These "video playback" monitors were present throughout production on the performance-capture stage. They existed for the actors and crew to see the "virtual action" so they might better understand how to adjust performances or better support the process.

ABOVE, BOTTOM: Cameron operates a swing cam.

giant movie lights, just a vast, empty space with a handful of guys hunched over their computers off to the side. The performance-capture Volume for *Avatar* measured roughly six times that of a typical motion-capture Volume, which would enable production to capture even large-scale action, such as riders on galloping horses and any manner of wire-rigged flying gags and other stunts. Giant Studios mounted 120 motion-capture cameras into a grid on the ceiling of the Playa Vista production stage, with each camera calibrated to feed the performance-capture data to a bank of computers and monitors on a platform at one end. "We needed that many cameras," explained Matt Madden, "because we were going to be covering a lot of space for things like horse runs and massive set pieces. We wanted to be

able to cover any possible combination of action with one setup. We wanted to be prepared for anything and not slow down production by having to do a camera change." The cameras themselves were commercially available black-and-white surveillance "smart cameras," with small computers connected to Giant's workstations. Rather than make image-processing adjustments to the cameras physically, Giant crew members could simply log in to any of the 120 cameras from a main computer and make the adjustment via an Ethernet connection.

The performance-capture setup also included HD monitors positioned around the Volume. *Avatar* was the first film production to establish an all-HD workflow, which would subsequently become standard operating

ABOVE: Cameron reviews the "quad-splits," in which four reference cam images are displayed on a single monitor.

OPPOSITE: Performance-capture session in progress in the Volume at Playa Vista, late May 2007. The Volume at Playa Vista was spacious enough for crowds of people, large stunt scenes, and even battle action with galloping horses. As seen here, the crew used a system of modular risers for rapid set changes. Note Cameron discussing the session with Laz Alonso between takes, in the lower-right-hand corner of the picture. (**LEFT**) Later, Cameron with the virtual camera. (**OVERLEAF, INSET**) Stunt performers ride through the Volume. Compare that image to the final frame grab of Alonso's performance as Tsu'Tey (**OVERLEAF**). The horses, as well as the props, were all fitted with retro-reflective markers so their motion could be captured, to give the final scene a feeling of natural movement.

ABOVE: Worthington as Jake during a live-action shoot at the Stone Street Studio's Ops Center set, Wellington, New Zealand (mid-November 2007).

OPPOSITE, TOP: Performance-capture session in mid-September 2007 at Playa Vista; OPPOSITE, BOTTOM: A frame grab of the same moment from the final rendered scene.

procedure for films. Manually operated HD cameras that would shoot reference material were time code–locked to the motion-capture cameras and the single video camera on the helmet rigs to ensure synchronization of all the disparate recordings of the performers.

Concurrent with the technical preparations for production, Cameron was making final casting decisions. His casting philosophy was the same as it had been for his previous films: He was less interested in casting bona fide movie stars than he was in casting good actors that were the right fit. "I don't think movies today are about movie stars," Jon Landau commented. "Jim has proven throughout his career that it is about finding the right performers to play the right roles. That's what we wanted to do with *Avatar*." Casting director Margery Simkin spent many months looking at prospective actors from all over the world, recording the most promising on video so that Cameron could review those tapes and narrow the field.

Finding an actor to portray Jake Sully was key, as it is through his eyes that *Avatar*'s entire story is told. Jake also undergoes the most dramatic change from the beginning of the film to the end, as he evolves from a cynical, dispirited mercenary to an enlightened leader who cares passionately about his cause. "The trick about Jake was not writing the character," Cameron admitted. "The trick was finding the guy to play him." After seeing hundreds of actors, Simkin called the filmmakers in June 2006 to tell them about an actor from Australia named Sam Worthington, then a complete unknown in the United States. Simkin reported that Worthington had "a visceral quality and would make audiences believe that people would follow him. There was an intelligence and intensity in his eyes that never wavered."

Intrigued, the producers offered Worthington an audition, but the actor was initially hesitant due to the secrecy surrounding the project. "I got a phone call to do this audition," Worthington recalled, "but they wouldn't tell me anything about the script or even who the director

was. And I thought, 'Well, here's another waste of my time.'" For his audition tape, Worthington played a scene in which Jake Sully meets a scientist in the Avatar program. As an actor read the scientist's lines off camera, Worthington laconically grunted "uh huh" every time the script called for Jake to say "yes." The Australian actor's tough-guy indifference, a reaction to feeling he was wasting his afternoon on another pointless audition, is what actually got him the job. A week later, Worthington received another phone call, this time informing him that it was a James Cameron project, and that Cameron himself wanted him to fly to Los Angeles to audition for him in person. "I told him he had me at 'uh huh,'" Cameron says. Once Worthington was stateside, the filmmakers worked with him in their Lightstorm offices. Then, in August, they flew him out again for an informal test with actress Zoë Saldana, who would play the Na'vi princess, Neytiri. Later still, the filmmakers did a full-blown, 3-D screen test with the actor. "We shot five scenes with Sam," Jon Landau recalled, "and we did that with a couple of other actors, as well. We did a scene from the beginning of the

movie, scenes from the middle of the movie, and a scene from the end of the movie. And while each actor was good in his own right, Sam was the one who nailed every scene. One of the hardest things to find in an actor of Sam's age is a combination of sensitivity, vulnerability, and strength, and Sam had all of that. In just watching these screen tests you got the evolution and the journey that the character goes on, and you wanted to go on that journey with him. As an audience, we want to stand by him and go fight with him as our leader in the third act of the film."

Ultimately, a long time would pass before the filmmakers made their final commitment to Worthington. "Poor Sam went through quite an ordeal with us," said Landau. "We first read him in June 2006, and we loved him then, but just because of the process of getting the movie going, we didn't make a final decision as to who we would cast in the part until January of 2007. To Sam's credit, he turned down other work, and said, 'No, *this* is the movie that I want to do.'"

An issue that stalled Worthington's final casting was his Australian accent, which Cameron joked was thicker than

Crocodile Dundee's. The filmmakers had to convince Twentieth Century Fox that the actor could rid himself of the accent with the help of a dialect coach, and that, in the end, he would be worth the extra trouble. "I lobbied for him strongly from the beginning," said Cameron, "because I just felt he had something that I hadn't seen before in a guy of that age. There was this amazing sense of not only authenticity, but just personal power in his voice and demeanor." Worthington put in many hours with the dialect coach, and then shot another screen test, which finally convinced the studio that Sam Worthington *was* Jake Sully.

There was some irony in the fact that by the time *Avatar* was released, Worthington had gained fame with American audiences for his leading role in McG's *Terminator Salvation* (2009), the fourth installment of the franchise first conceived by James Cameron.

Zoë Saldana, too, would be cast as Neytiri as a relative unknown, and then make her mark in another film just months before *Avatar*'s release, portraying a young Uhura in J. J. Abrams's retooled *Star Trek* (2009). To Cameron's mind, Saldana was the embodiment of Neytiri as he had envisioned her, possessing the character's combination of delicacy and fierceness. "We did a screen test with her in August 2006," recalled Cameron, "and we committed to her soon after."

Due to years of professional dance training, Saldana also possessed a fine-tuned physicality and grace that would serve her well in the role. Once on the performance-capture stage, Saldana would be leaping, running, jumping, and swinging from simulated vines—essentially everything Neytiri does in the film. Saldana relished the opportunity to play such a physical character, to bring her body, as well as her mind and imagination, into a role, and

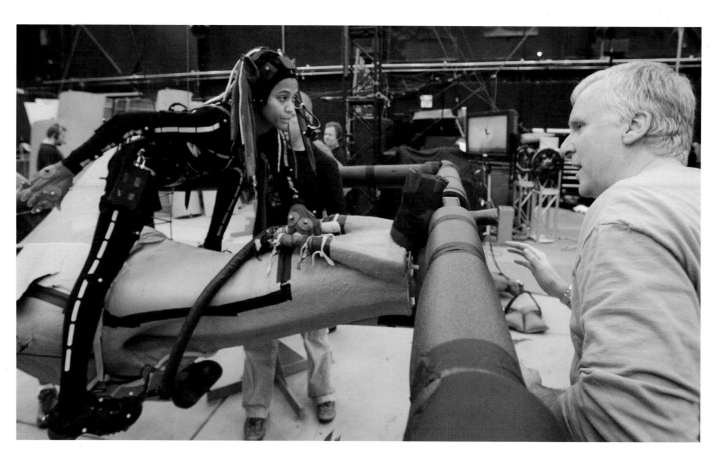

Casting an actress for the part of Neytiri, the Na'vi princess, was a task Cameron and Landau pursued in earnest for many months. A relative unknown at the time, Saldana's dance training was a compelling factor for the physical agility and grace required of the character. Once the female lead was in place, many elements of the production could begin moving forward.

OPPOSITE: Neytiri with Tse'zey, her banshee, in the eyrie of Hometree (frame grab).

ABOVE: Cameron directing Saldana during a performance-capture banshee ride session in the Volume at Playa Vista in mid-June 2007.

ABOVE: Weaver adjacent to an image of her character, Dr. Grace Augustine, on set at Playa Vista in late March 2007.

OPPOSITE, TOP: Shortly after the cast was finalized (early February 2007), Cameron gathered the actors for a read-through of the script.

OPPOSITE, BOTTOM: Later that year, actor Wes Studi (Eytukan) during a performance-capture session with Alonso (Tsu'Tey) and members of the core team of stunt players and performance-capture actors called "the troupe," playing Omaticaya clan members. Later in the production, it became possible to capture as many as sixteen characters at once. This still wasn't enough to do large crowds, so the entire troupe would be captured several times, in different parts of the set, and these separate "crowd tiles" were pieced together to create crowds of hundreds of people.

she trained for months to learn archery and styles of movement that were idiosyncratic to the Na'vi. "Zoë embraced Neytiri," said Cameron, "from learning the [Na'vi] language to practicing the movement skills to having her own thoughts and philosophies about the Na'vi people and how they live. Even before she knew she had the part, she was all about becoming a Na'vi."

The talents of Worthington and Saldana, separately, were essential to *Avatar*, but so, too, was their connection as a couple, that unquantifiable factor that makes for emotional and sexual spark as two actors perform a scene. Even though audiences would never see Worthington and Saldana together in their human forms, chemistry of the Kate Winslet–Leonardo DiCaprio kind was imperative. "Zoë and Sam had the same on-screen chemistry that we

were able to capture in a bottle on *Titanic*," said Jon Landau. "We were very fortunate."

Another leading role was that of Dr. Grace Augustine, an eighteen-year veteran of the avatar program and Jake's tough-talking, cigarette-smoking mentor. Grace epitomized the strong female roles in all of Cameron's films, a lineage that started with Sarah Connor in *The Terminator* and—later—*Terminator 2*, continued with Ripley in *Aliens*, and extended through Lindsey Brigman in *The Abyss* and Helen Tasker in *True Lies* (1994). Sigourney Weaver, who had played Ripley in all four *Alien* films, appreciated Cameron's penchant for writing women that were more Rambo than bimbo; noting that both Cameron and outer space had been very good to her, she signed on to play Grace in *Avatar*.

Surprisingly, Cameron initially hesitated to approach Weaver about the role, in part because she had worked with him so memorably on *Aliens* and he wanted *Avatar* to stand on its own. But as he looked at the character of Grace and considered the strength—both physical and intellectual—that would have to be brought to the role, he quickly realized that no one was a better fit than Sigourney Weaver. The only question was whether Weaver would deem *Avatar* a fit for her. "We reached out to her," said Landau, "thinking she might not be interested in doing this type of movie. But she read the script and saw how each and every character that Jim wrote, including Grace, had a full arc—and she fell in love with it. We were blessed to have her with us."

Joel David Moore was cast as Norm, a scientist whose acceptance into the avatar program is the realization of a lifelong dream. Norm, Grace, and Jake represented the characters that would be seen both in human form and as CG avatars. Among the supporting characters that would be seen *only* as live-action persons was Colonel Quaritch, the leader of the RDA's military force, played by Stephen Lang. "You believe this is a guy who has been on Pandora for fifteen-plus years," Landau remarked. "He's seen the worst of it on Earth, and he's seen even worse on Pandora, and yet he's the one surviving. He's our General Patton."

As the corporate administrator Parker Selfridge, Giovanni Ribisi brought a sense of humor to the role the film-

ABOVE: Cast as Norm Spellman, actor Joel David Moore on set in New Zealand, late January 2008.

RIGHT: Actor Giovanni Ribisi, cast as RDA administrator Parker Selfridge, practicing his character's golf swing in the Ops Center set at Stone Street Studios in New Zealand, late October 2007.

makers hadn't realized existed, making him a real person rather than just a corporate stooge. Similarly, Michelle Rodriguez brought complexity to her role as the marine pilot Trudy Chacon. The filmmakers looked at many actresses for the role, even though "Michelle Rodriguez" had been the *first* name to come to mind. "The role hadn't really been fleshed out in the first draft of the script," explained Landau, "and so we didn't think it was a role she would embrace. But we went to her anyway, and it turned out that she is a *huge* science-fiction fan. She loved the part." With Rodriguez on board, Cameron embellished Trudy in his screenplay, giving her more of a character arc.

Just as important as the live-action performers were those who would appear only in their roles as Na'vi. In addition to Zoë Saldana, they included Wes Studi as the patriarch Eytukan, CCH Pounder as the spiritual leader Mo'at, and Laz Alonso as the warrior Tsu'Tey. In casting the Na'vi roles, the filmmakers were most emphatically *not* merely casting voices. Through performance capture, the totality of the actors' performances—their voices and their physicality, their facial expressions, and their emotional states—would all be there in the final CG characters, a point Cameron and Landau emphasized when approaching the actors.

"When you see the performance of Mo'at in the movie," said Landau, "there's no mistaking that it's CCH Pounder who's creating that performance. Same thing with Wes Studi and Laz Alonso. Their performances came through just

ABOVE: Actress Michelle Rodriguez, cast to play Samson pilot Trudy Chacon, early December 2007.

LEFT: Actor Stephen Lang plays the formidable Colonel Miles Quaritch.

like Jack Nicholson's did as the Joker or Jim Carrey's did as the Grinch. We were just using synthetic characters instead of prosthetics." To qualm any fears the actors might have that their performances would be lost in the CG characters, Landau and Cameron showed them the original 2005 prototype scene, which brilliantly illustrated how true the final CG scene was to the original performances. "We wanted them to know that, at the end of the day, when they looked up on the screen, they would see themselves."

With the final casting of the Na'vi and avatar roles, the tech team launched the full-scale construction of the helmet-camera rigs the actors would wear while performing on the performance-capture stage. To ensure a custom fit, Stan Winston Studio took traditional life casts of each actor—which would also be used in refining the character designs—and made fiberglass shells from those, lined and covered in foam to make them more comfortable for the performers. Glenn Derry's team built the technical aspects of the head rigs, including the standard-definition video cameras that would be mounted to the miniature boom

arms. After working out all of the specs in a prototype, Derry and his crew went into production of fifty head-rig units—enough for the lead actors, their stunt doubles, and the performers who would play background Na'vi.

Final casting decisions also led to a redesign of the Na'vi and avatar characters so that they would resemble the specific actors portraying them. The previous year, the filmmakers had tasked Stan Winston Studio with developing and refining the nascent Na'vi and avatar designs that had been sketched out by Cameron and the concept artists. Stan Winston, with whom Cameron had been close since their collaboration on *The Terminator*, had left the daily running of his venerated studio to lead supervisors since contracting multiple myeloma in 2001, but he took early meetings with Cameron and Landau for *Avatar*, a project for which he had much enthusiasm—but would not live to see completed. Winston passed away on June 15, 2008, a year and a half before the film's release.

Winston supervisor John Rosengrant, too, had worked with Cameron since *The Terminator*, and the studio's

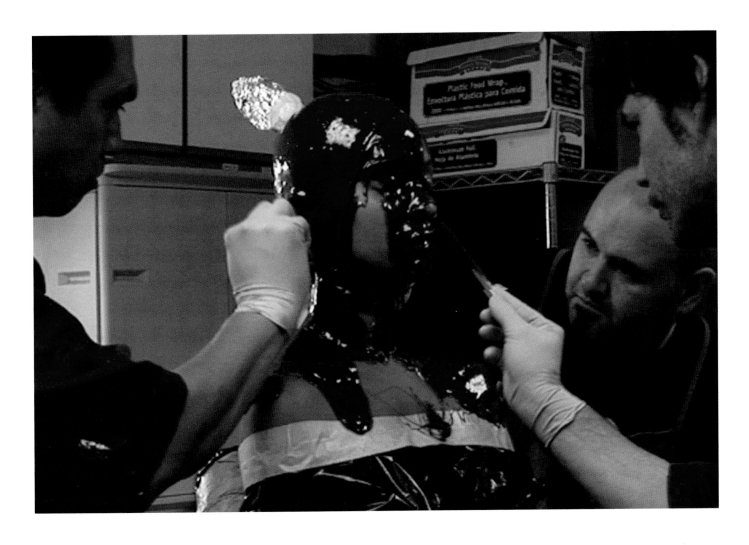

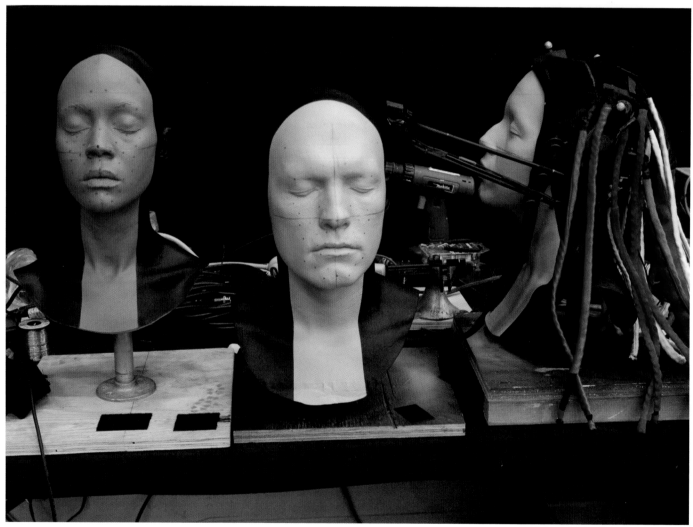

Once the actors were chosen, Stan Winston Studio embarked on several techniques in the process of infusing the Na'vi and the avatars with the actors' looks and characteristics. First, Winston Studio artists molded traditional life casts of the leading actors, including Saldana (OPPOSITE); these casts were used in the creation of physical busts (OVERLEAF) as well as head rigs (ABOVE, BOTTOM). Including the sampling seen here, fifty of these personalized head rigs were produced by Glenn Derry and worn by the actors throughout production.

ABOVE, TOP: Winston Studio conducted tests of the characters' facial expressions in ZBrush. They photographed the actors in various facial movements, including their most extreme expressions, and then studied how the character would look with the same expressions applied (as seen here, with Saldana's expressions mapped to Neytiri). Since the nose and brow regions of the Na'vi faces were quite different from the actors', it was necessary to figure out how wrinkles and muscle deformation would work during strong emotional states.

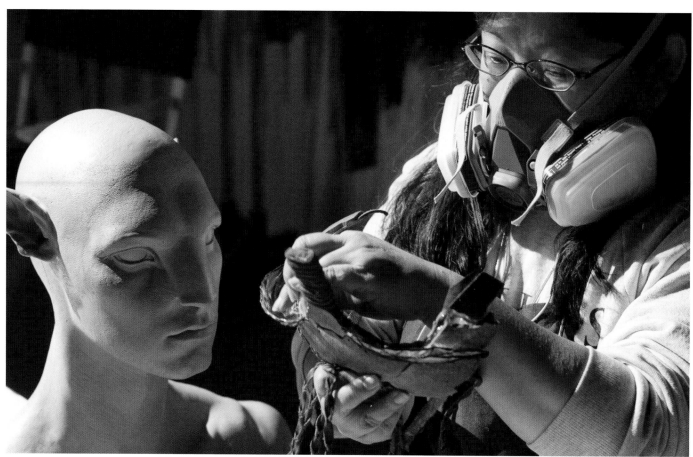

OPPOSITE, TOP: Finished head busts by Stan Winston Studio; ultraviolet paint and lighting were used to simulate the glowing patterns of bioluminescent dots.

OPPOSITE, BOTTOM: A Winston Studio review session in late April 2007. Present are Rick Carter, Rey Perez, Scott Patton, Joey Orosco, Joseph Pepe, John Rosengrant, Neville Page, and Cameron, reviewing the busts shown in the above image.

ABOVE, TOP LEFT: A final resin bust of Neytiri.

ABOVE, TOP RIGHT: One of SWS's designs for Neytiri's ceremonial body paint.

ABOVE, BOTTOM: Bust in production; here, a costume crew member puts together Jake's avatar's banshee visor.

many contributions to *Avatar* were left in his capable hands. "Stan Winston Studio had a multitude of roles on this movie," noted Jon Landau. "They were first and foremost responsible for the character designs, but they are also the ones who built our AMP Suit. To have the ability to do something that is so organic and something that is so high-tech, all in the same facility, is rather remarkable. John Rosengrant and his team tackled both with vim and vigor."

The Winston team spent its initial time on the project—prior to final casting—refining the generic look of the Na'vi by scanning photographs of real people into the computer and manipulating them in Photoshop to incorporate Na'vi features, such as the large amber eyes and leonine noses. The Winston artists also employed Photoshop to create varieties of cyan colorations and stripe patterns for the Na'vi flesh. "We gave Jim many, many variations of paint schemes and color schemes," recalled John Rosengrant. "We came up with probably twenty-five different iterations. One would be a little more blue, another more gray, and each had a different stripe pattern and pattern of

bioluminescence. We tweaked the noses, the color of the eyes—some were more yellow, some less. These differences from one iteration to the next were extremely subtle, but what is amazing about Jim is that he saw those differences immediately. Jim is such a well-rounded artist, he could pick up on the most subtle change." Presented with the many Photoshop renderings, Cameron eventually narrowed the options and chose the colorations, patterns, and facial characteristics that best represented each character.

Throughout 2006 and beyond, Stan Winston Studio artists began incorporating the now-cast actors' specific facial characteristics into their Na'vi and avatar designs. The Winston crew photographed the actors striking a variety of poses and making different facial expressions, and then married those images to the Na'vi and avatar characters. "We found that the best way to convey the essence of the actor's performance," Jon Landau commented, "and the best way for us to see if we were really getting that performance in our CG character, was to bring in similarities in the faces. We had to recognize Sam Worthington, Sigourney Weaver, and Joel David Moore in their avatars." The

Winston artists surrounded the Na'vi eyes of the avatars, for example, with the corresponding area of the actors' eyes, including their brow line. They also incorporated the actors' mouths into the characters so that their lip and tongue movement when speaking dialogue would correlate to the speaking CG avatar.

The Winston designers had the most difficulty incorporating Sigourney Weaver's features into their avatar design, partly due to the fact that her avatar was supposed to be eighteen years younger than Grace appears in her live-action scenes. Rather than go off current reference, the artists imported fifteen-year-old photographs of the actress. "To de-age Grace's avatar," said John Rosengrant, "we took pictures of Sigourney Weaver from *Alien 3* [1992] and brought them into ZBrush. Then we started sculpting and pushing things around to create her avatar." Artists found that the avatar was not suitably recognizable as Sigourney Weaver once they added the broad Na'vi nose, because it was so at odds with Weaver's naturally slim, patrician nose. After exploring several options, the designers finally decided to give Grace's avatar a more human-size nose than her avatar colleagues, justified by the logic that the mix of human and Na'vi DNA could result in any number of different facial-feature combinations.

Though it was a more subtle effect, the Winston artists incorporated actors' facial features even in the pure Na'vi characters. "We never see human counterparts for the Na'vi characters, of course," stated Jon Landau, "but even there, we integrated some of the features of the actors portraying them. If you know Wes Studi, you recognize him as the patriarch of the Na'vi clan. You recognize CCH Pounder in Mo'at. You recognize Zoë Saldana in Neytiri. You can definitely see it. Again, it was the best way to make sure that the actors' performances were coming through in the CGI characters."

OPPOSITE, LEFT: A series of four angles on the clay sculpts of Jake, incorporating Worthington's features. These busts, which preceded the skin coloring, also present the look of newly woven hair designs.

OPPOSITE, RIGHT: The final, painted bust of Jake, by Winston Studio. Once the clay sculpts had been approved, they were cast; this final resin bust is made from the resulting molds with hair and coloring applied.

ABOVE, TOP: Actor Joel David Moore undergoing a few stages of the design process by Winston Studio. From left to right: being prepared for a 3-D laser scan of his head; a CG model based on Joel's features; paint-over of a render; a three-quarter-view render with hair. Simultaneously, Weta Digital was also collecting facial data. By combining this and referring to the Winston Studio artwork seen on these pages as a visual guide, the Weta artists began refining the look of the Na'vi and avatar characters.

ABOVE, BOTTOM: A frame grab from the film and an example of Norm's avatar's final look; he is flying in the body of the Samson—looking out at the Pandoran landscape for the first time.

ABOVE and OPPOSITE: Clay sculptures, called "maquettes," of the characters and creatures of Pandora on display in the Lightstorm conference room. Along the back row are resin busts of the main characters.

The Winston team also made human-size busts of all the characters, either from scans or traditional life casts of the actors. "There were many ways to do this," Rosengrant commented, "but it seemed most efficient to take a life cast of the actor, do a clay press-out, and sculpt the character on top of that." The final busts were full-scale in that they were *human*-size, but they were not true Na'vi-size. "By making them human-size, we could make the busts directly from the life casts, rather than having to scale them up."

The Winston team created human-scale full-body Na'vi and avatar models to provide Cameron with tangible figures that he could study in real-world, rather than digital-world, lighting. "Looking at a computer model just isn't the same as looking at a physical one," Rosengrant said.

"With these models, Jim could look at a whole character and move lights around it. It helped everyone to envision what the character would look like." Toward that same end, a Winston makeup artist painted blue-tinted makeup onto a small group of very tall, thin performers. Those performers moved about an exterior environment to give Cameron a rough idea of how ambulatory Na'vi might look in different lighting scenarios, as they moved from sunlight to shadow, for example, or from day to night.

The next step for the Winston crew was to create larger, full-scale Na'vi models, which would stand ten feet tall. These models didn't resemble any of the lead characters, but were, rather, generic representations of the Na'vi. Throughout production, these models were on set to help

Cameron and the actors determine eyelines and otherwise visualize how tall a real Na'vi or avatar might be in a shot. "I'm sure it was helpful to the actors, visually, to be able to see what they would be working with in final shots," said Rosengrant. All the busts and models were scanned, which produced 3-D data that Weta Digital would use in building the CG Na'vi and avatars.

To lend design support to the artists at Lightstorm, Stan Winston Studio also rendered some refinements for the viperwolf. Winston artists devised paint schemes in Photoshop and employed ZBrush to sculpt a final viperwolf model. One of the details the team worked out was the mechanism by which the viperwolf's jaw would go from a closed position to an open one, revealing many rows of long, sharp teeth. "We built a 3-D model of the mouth in ZBrush and really put it through its paces," said Rosengrant. "And we did all of that with Jim, on the fly. We were able to make quick changes that Jim wanted right then. We had a lot of two- or three-hour sessions with Jim during this process, working on this and other characters on the computer." The approved 3-D viperwolf sculpt was replicated in a clay sculpture, which, again, was scanned to provide Weta with 3-D data.

Rosengrant and the Winston Studio crew refined the design of the direhorse, as well, using ZBrush computer drawings and old-school clay sculptures to create the creature's overlapping scales, massively armored shoulders and hindquarters, and rows of breathing apertures called "spiracles," complete with valvelike "opercula."

Stan Winston Studio was also responsible for construction of the full-size practical AMP Suit. Working with Cameron, TyRuben Ellingson had designed the AMP Suit in a rough 3-D animation that illustrated how the various parts would move. The Winston crew then developed the AMP Suit's mechanical engineering in more detail so they could build a functioning model in full scale. Winston artists remodeled the AMP Suit in their 3-D modeling program and took it apart in the computer to clarify the separate elements that would have to be built. To test basic functions and ensure that the cockpit would accommodate a performer, the Winston team built a foam-core-and-wood mock-up of the AMP Suit and put one of its crew members inside. In a test run for Jim Cameron, the Winston crew operated the mock-up using telemetry devices from previous projects. "Jim even climbed inside the mock-up to try it out for himself," Rosengrant recalled.

Having determined that the basic concept was workable, Rosengrant and his crews carved custom-designed nuts, bolts, and other detailing—inspired by reference photographs of military hardware, Abrams tanks, and Apache helicopters—into the mock-up's foam. The team then molded individual parts and cast them out of fiberglass, supported with aluminum and steel. "There were around three hundred parts—maybe more," said Rosengrant. "The AMP Suit was an enormous job. It was thirteen and a half feet tall and weighed twelve hundred pounds, total. It was so complex, we actually made up an official military manual for the thing, and sent it over to Jon Landau!"

Back at Lightstorm, where Robert Stromberg and his team of artists were continuing to design all the elements of Pandora's rain forest, the virtual-art department began

ABOVE: Rosengrant trying out the AMP Suit during construction at SWS.

ABOVE, INSET: A close-up on the AMP Suit's palm shows the level of detail and engineering that went into the design effort.

OPPOSITE: The AMP Suit was shipped from California to New Zealand; here, Lang is shown trying it on for size, early November 2007.

building computer models based on those environmental designs. "Just like on a normal production," said Jon Landau, "we had to hire a construction crew. But instead of hiring people with hammers and nails like you normally would, we hired computer artists, and these artists had to create our world in the computer for us before we could go on to the virtual-production stage."

In addition to building environments for specific scenes, the digital artists built a library of trees, plants, waterways, mountains, hills, vines, and brush—everything imaginable—so that Cameron could pick and choose from those elements and build up a setting to his liking when it came time to shoot any given scene. The team also began building character and creature models based on the concept art. "We started manufacturing digital assets—characters, environments, hardware, everything," said Nolan Murtha. "Any and all of these assets were available to Jim at a moment's notice."

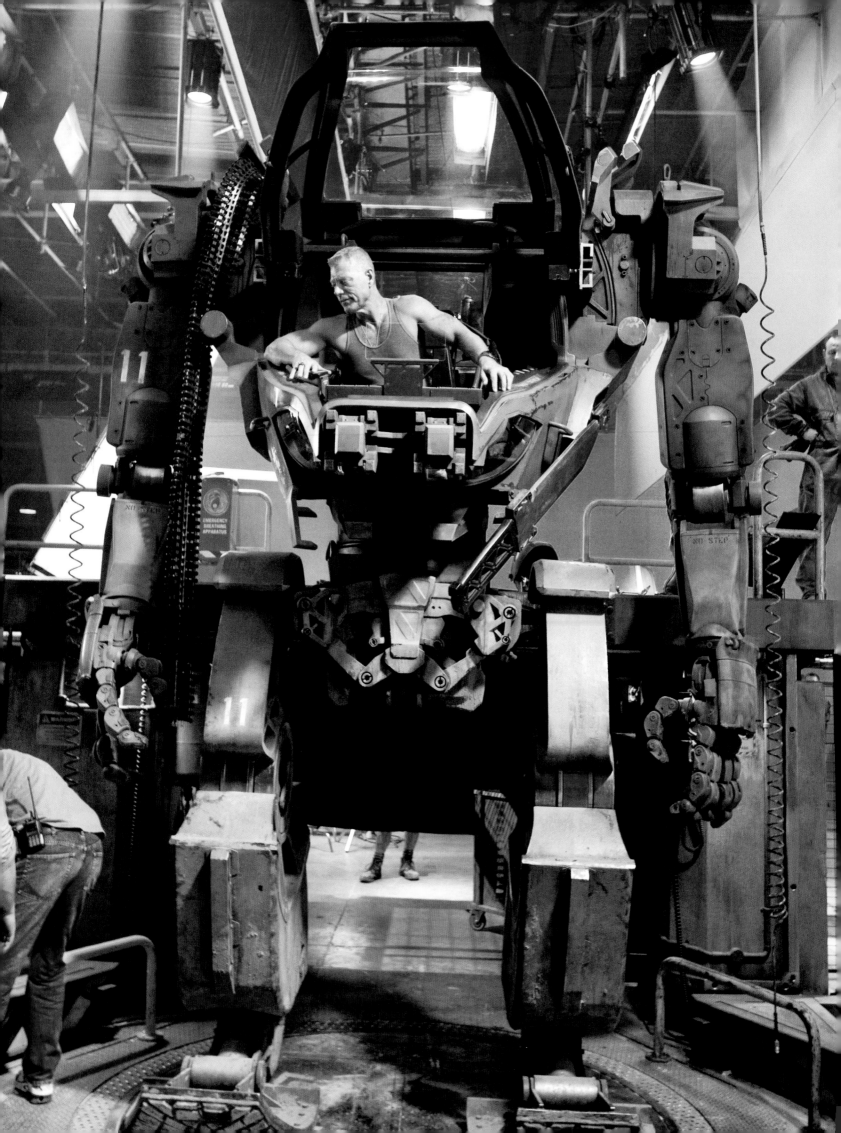

The building of these digital assets, which would number in the thousands, was a project that would consume the virtual-art department for nearly two years. Though these assets would not be rendered out to their final photo-realistic look at this point, they were structurally accurate representations of the CG models that would, eventually, come out of Weta Digital in their final shots.

By late fall 2006, production had gathered at least some of the "stuff"—digital assets, technical hardware, and applicable software—needed to begin making the film. The actors would not be called for many weeks, but the system was sufficiently up and running to enable the filmmakers to begin motion-capturing stunts and aircraft within the Playa Vista Volume, executing the latter using scaled models of the film's various helicopters and ships. James Cameron and Richard Baneham would hold these models in their hands, and then "fly" them through the air to capture flight paths and maneuvers. Ramps on the stage enabled them to simulate aircraft ascents and descents. "We even had two professional stunt helicopter pilots there to help us," Baneham recalled. "They slapped our

wrists if we didn't vector properly as we puppeteered aircraft through the scene. And we could see the CG aircraft moving through the CG environment on the stage monitors, 100 percent real time, all the time."

All the flying vehicles, from the agile Scorpion gunships to the massive Dragon, were captured by hand-flying wireframe models. Cameron drew on his experience as a helicopter pilot to create accurate flight dynamics for these futuristic rotorcraft. From subtle wobbles in hover through high-performance aerobatics in battle, all the flying vehicles were manually performed to behave like real rotorcraft, with special attention to the sense of mass and momentum that is often missing from CG aircraft. Later, this captured motion would be turned into highly realistic animation with articulation of the rotor systems and flight control surfaces. These duties were divided between Weta and ILM, with the latter taking many of the hard-surface model CG scenes later in the production.

There was a steep learning curve as the "pilots" tested how best to puppeteer appropriate flight dynamics, especially those for aerial skirmishes in the final battle. Early on,

OPPOSITE, LEFT: Cameron operates the first virtual camera during one of the capture sessions at Playa Vista, mid-August 2006.

OPPOSITE, RIGHT: Baneham puppeteers, while the captured banshee movement is displayed on the monitor, mid-June 2007.

ABOVE, TOP: Concept painting by Cole—an initial depiction of Jake and Neytiri being chased by the leonopteryx.

ABOVE, BOTTOM: Baneham and Cameron enact flight maneuvers in the Volume. Baneham is holding a dragon; Cameron is flying a Samson and a Scorpion.

the crew tried to capture as many as five aircraft models at once, each with its own puppeteer, but with so many bodies onstage, the scene began to resemble a Keystone Kops routine. Learning from that mistake, the crew broke up large-scale, multiple-ship aerial action into smaller pieces for motion-capture purposes, and then layered those separate passes together to achieve the final epic battle scene.

The creature flight scenes would turn out to be the most difficult type of scene encountered in virtual production. It took many months to perfect the technique of capturing the flight dynamics of the creatures, then integrating the movements of the Na'vi riders, and finally creating the aturalistic aerial cameras necessary to make it all seem real.

Cameron and Richie Baneham spent many sessions evolving the method for capturing the flying creatures like the banshees and leonopteryx. Two scales of model creatures were used in the Volume, both fashioned from bent wire. The smaller-scale banshee, ¼ inch to the foot, was used for flight paths with large vertical displacements, such as climbs and dives, because it was more difficult for Cameron and Baneham to fly the models by hand vertically than to move around the stage horizontally. They would often find themselves walking down from high ramps, then bending down to fly the creature close to the stage floor, to get the total vertical displacement necessary.

When more subtle control of wing movement was necessary, ½ inch to the foot models were used. Cameron and Baneham found that the wire models could be used to create very natural movements of the creatures along their flight paths, but it took many hours of practice to learn the correct relationship between forward travel and banking of the wings. Pitch, yaw, and roll all had a specific relationship to forward speed, such as speed slowing in a climb and increasing in a dive. Cameron found that by keeping a rhythmic count in his head, like the ticking of a metronome, he was able to walk at an even pace, and therefore capture exactly the right ratio between banking and forward speed. In the end, Baneham and Cameron captured every bit of flying motion by hand, for all the flying creatures.

All of this preproduction capture, though useful, represented only a fraction of what Cameron had wanted to do when planning the *Avatar* shoot. Initially, he had intended to motion-capture a large percentage of the film's sequences with stunt doubles for an entire six months prior to production. Streaming that capture data to the crude digital figures, Cameron could do camera moves, work out composition issues, and determine exact digital environments and backgrounds. In a sense, the preproduction team would be shooting templates for shots, working out every detail in advance, and then, when the actors came in, all of those decisions would have been made. Precapture would have increased the efficiency and speed of the final performance-capture sessions, enabling Cameron and the actors to concentrate solely on performance, but, unfortunately, there were still too many glitches in the virtual-production technology to make the preshoot blocking and capture sessions feasible.

While crews prepared for production on the performance-capture stage, lead actors endured a kind of military boot-camp training in which, among other things, they learned to handle both the low-tech Na'vi weapons, such as knives and spears, and the more high-tech guns and rocket launchers of the Hell's Gate team. The actors took archery lessons, learned to ride horses, and were trained in hand-to-hand combat, as well. Stephen Lang was trained to work the controls of the AMP Suit as though he'd been doing it his whole life, and Michelle Rodriguez put in twelve hours of helicopter flight training in the skies over Los Angeles to lend credence to shots of Trudy piloting her transport craft. To prepare for his performance of Jake, Sam Worthington had the additional challenge of going through a condensed but intense Marine boot camp training with Cameron's brother, John David, who is a former Marine.

During the training period, Na'vi actors also worked with Cirque du Soleil performer Terry Notary to develop a vocabulary of movements that was uniquely Na'vi, but inspired by real-world indigenous peoples, as well as large cats and primates. "We worked to answer questions like, 'How would the Na'vi touch?'" Notary said. "'How would they move when they're happy? And how would they use their tails?'" Choreographer Lula Washington also developed celebratory Na'vi dance moves, which were executed by leading Na'vi performers or by dancers from her dance-theater troupe, who portrayed background members of the Omaticaya clan.

"There were several major scenes involving choreography," said Cameron, "including a huge festival after the "sturmbeest hunt" and, later in the story, the preparation

ABOVE, TOP: While Cameron checks the action in the virtual camera, stunt performers climb the last rock of the "Beanstalk" and jump to vines dangling from a passing floating mountain. Note the stagehands rocking the large setpiece to simulate the effect of the Na'vis' weight tipping the floating boulder they are climbing across.

ABOVE, BOTTOM LEFT: Stuntman Ilram Choi, doubling for Laz Alonso, leaps to a rope, which stands in for a vine. The nearby monitor (ABOVE, BOTTOM RIGHT) simultaneously displays a virtual view of his "real-time character" doing the same action in the world of Pandora.

Before actual shooting started, Cameron brought the actors to the jungles of Hawaii.

ABOVE, TOP: Worthington and Saldana practicing shooting with a bow and arrow. To add more originality to the Na'vi, it was later decided to invert the bow hand so that the palm was facing out.

ABOVE, BOTTOM LEFT: Saldana drinking water from a leaf. This image was later referenced for lighting and water dynamics in what ultimately became a brief scene in the film in which Neytiri drinks from a Pandoran flower. This shot won Weta Digital the 8th Annual Visual Effects Society Award for Best Single Visual Effect of the Year, 2009.

ABOVE, BOTTOM RIGHT: Cameron and Weaver at a cast dinner the first night in Hawaii.

on the eve of battle. But unfortunately these scenes were removed from the release version of the film and can only be seen in the special edition DVD and Blu-ray. Lula's troupe, however, were important in creating a unified sense of culturally specific physicality to the Na'vi in many scenes that remain in the film, including the ceremonies to resurrect Grace and Jake. For example, Mo'at's "voodoo priestess" movements at the ceremonies were created by Lula and performed by her daughter, Tamika, doubling for CCH Pounder.

Na'vi and avatar cast members with speaking roles also had to take classes to learn the Na'vi language, invented by linguist Dr. Paul Frommer. When hiring Frommer for the job, Cameron had asked him to create a language with words that would be relatively easy to pronounce, but entirely unlike any known human language. Frommer devised a vocabulary of approximately one thousand Na'vi words, which the actors learned phonetically and memorized for dialogue scenes. "Paul Frommer did a phenomenal job writing a Na'vi language," commented Jon Landau, "and the cast embraced the idea of learning this language."

"It was all about giving Jim options," said Frommer, "and then we locked in the language's structural properties, pronunciation rules, and how the words were built." The names of characters in Cameron's script—Neytiri and Tsu'Tey and Mo'at—suggested a Polynesian or Indonesian influence, and Frommer invented sounds similar to what would be heard in the languages from those regions. "To add some spice to it," Frommer said, "we decided on some popping sounds, what linguists call 'ejectives,' such as *p* and *t* and *k*. We also came up with combinations of sounds that don't exist in English or other Western languages—combinations like *fta,* and *fko.*" There is also a range of sounds utterly absent from the Na'vi language. "There's no *sh* or *ch,* for example. It wasn't just a question of the sounds themselves, but how they fit together."

Though the Na'vi language doesn't assign words gender, as in French or Spanish, there are distinct forms for words pertaining to male and female. The word for "brother," for example, is *tsmukan,* while the word for "sister" is *tsmukeh;* "*-an* is a masculine ending, and *-eh* is a feminine ending," said Frommer. "That was something Jim actually came up with, and I expanded on the idea."

In addition to learning the alien language, the actors worked with dialect coach Carla Meyer to fine-tune a distinct Na'vi accent when speaking English. The most difficult

thing for Zoë Saldana, who had far more lines of dialogue than any of the other actors performing Na'vi characters, was speaking her English lines with a Na'vi "accent" that didn't slip into a familiar dialect such as French or Italian. Sam Worthington's challenge was that he was not only learning Na'vi, but he was learning to speak in an American, rather than Australian, accent. "It was like learning two languages," Worthington commented, "and the Na'vi was easier than the American accent!" Crew members picked up some Na'vi through the course of production, and would throw out pejoratives such as *skxawng*—which means "moron"— to tease one another on the set.

Just prior to the start of production, Cameron took his well-trained cast and members of the crew up into the mountains of Hawaii, where they spent their days and nights trekking through the tropical forest, bow-hunting, building campfires, even cooking food wrapped in leaves buried in the ground—anything that might simulate the Na'vi-jungle experience. Cameron wanted the cast to have a visceral memory of what it was like to move through thick foliage, since there would be no such greenery on the performance-capture stage. "We had to live without sophisticated technology, tools, and comforts," Saldana recalled of the experience. "I was almost naked for three days, digging and climbing and muddy like a dead rat." Later, when she was acting on the performance-capture stage, Saldana was grateful to have had the experience. "On this bare stage, which had no sets, we had to act as if we were in Pandora's mud, water, humidity, trees, elevation—everything. Being in Hawaii gave us a mental imprint on which we could draw when we had to simulate an action on the virtual stage."

Cameron and second unit director Steve Quale also shot hours of HD reference footage of the actors moving through the rain forest, drinking from leaves, cooking, and even shots of a bulldozer clearing the jungle that they happened upon. This footage became invaluable later in re-creating the rain forest in CG. "The hours of HD reference shot in Hawaii helped enormously in the years of work that followed," said Cameron, "in the creation of the photo-real world of Pandora."

With the return of the cast and crew from Hawaii, the filmmakers conducted a few short tests with Sam Worthington and Zoë Saldana to ensure their digital models were appropriately calibrated to their bodies.

And with that, the first virtual production of a feature film in movie history was ready to commence.

THREE

TÌSPSE'E: CAPTURE

A form of entertainment that became popular in the 1960s was "black-box" theater, so named because it consisted of performers in a room with black walls and a flat floor, with little in the way of set dressing, lighting, costuming, or other theatrical accoutrements to distract from raw performance. The performance-capture Volume in Playa Vista, where much of *Avatar* was created, was, essentially, black-box cinema. Despite all of the technical paraphernalia that went into the setup, when actors stepped within the Volume, performance was paramount, and most of the peripheral elements of typical movie production were absent. "We didn't have a director of photography; we didn't have a gaffer; we didn't have *any* of that," said Jon Landau.

Cameron, first assistant directors Josh McLaglen and Maria Battle Campbell, the virtual-production crews, and the actors would be in that black box for a total of about two and a half years, off and on. They got off to a rocky start as they struggled to work out the myriad problems of virtual production. "As successful and enlightening as the prototype test was," Jon Landau noted, "it misled us into thinking that all scenes could be done as easily as the prototype was. Unfortunately, we found out that this was not true. Scenes with four people were much more complicated than scenes with two people—and scenes with large numbers of extras were a whole new challenge. There were

OPPOSITE: Worthington, Saldana, and Alonso on a riser in the Volume, late August 2007.

two things that Jim said all along the way. One was, 'You know we're breaking new ground, because we are screwing up so much.' The other was, 'We won't solve our last problem with the process until our very last day on the film.'"

"We'd stop in the middle of the day," recalled Cameron, "and sit down at a table in the middle of the stage and try to figure out how to do it, because we'd hit a wall. We would shoot in fits and starts. We'd shoot a bit, then go figure out more stuff, and then we'd shoot a bit more. It was very exploratory. I've always tried to push the envelope, but this time it pushed back, so we had to push harder. I liken the experience of making *Avatar* to jumping off a cliff and knitting the parachute on the way down."

By the time *Avatar* was a year into production, the worst of the kinks of virtual production had been worked out, and the process was proceeding in a series of more or less predictable steps. Typically, a month or two in advance of shooting a performance-capture scene, the virtual-art department would be provided with the slate of upcoming scenes to allow them to pull and prepare the appropriate

digital environments. Early in production, Cameron had attempted to shoot his performance capture with these raw digital sets streamed into his virtual camera. But unresolved digital environment issues led to frequent—and frustrating—delays in shooting scenes. Rather than lose that time waiting for problems with the digital environments to be sorted out, Cameron set up a new chain of events in which first assistant director Josh McLaglen would do a "prescout" on the raw set that had come from the virtual-art department to ensure that all the scene requirements were present. If the scene called for a character to trip on a tree root, McLaglen would make sure that tree and that root were there, in their appropriate forms. If a scene called for action in water, McLaglen made sure water was present.

Cameron would then "scout" the digital environment and dress it out with additional plants, vines, or other elements. "You know how on a live-action production you'll have a 'greens department?'" queried Jon Landau. "Well, we had a greens department, too—a whole library of stuff that we could use to dress any shot. You

ABOVE: Jake's avatar standing in front of a grove of helicoradians, not yet aware that a hammerhead stands behind them (frame grab).

could say, 'I want more of those purple spirally things but make them bigger, and make them blue, instead.' We could change the color, the size, the way a certain plant tilted, how tall it was, and we could bring any combination of that to any shot."

The dressed-out digital environments would then go to two departments: the digital-model department and the staging department. From its library of digital assets, the digital-model department would pull the additional environmental dressing elements, plus all the characters, hardware, and props used in the scene. The staging department, meanwhile, would assemble corresponding set pieces on the stage floor so that the performers could physically interact with their environment. "If there was a hillside in the virtual world," Matt Madden explained, "we would put a little wooden-slope structure out there for the actor to walk up. We wanted all those set pieces there so the actors or stunt doubles wouldn't have to fake any of the action. The actor could just concentrate on acting out the character in the environment, and we were responsible for making it look right in the virtual world."

"One of the first hurdles that had to be overcome," said Cameron, "was the fact that the jungle is not flat like the stage floor. A virtual set cannot support a physical actor—they'll just walk right through it—so if the scene called for hilly terrain, virtual terrain needed to be duplicated with contoured structures that the actors could walk on. Virtual production was so new that there was no existing system for doing this. It had to be invented."

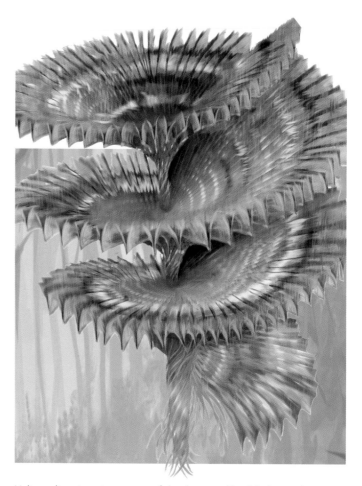

Helicoradians in various stages of development. The 2-D designs (ABOVE, BOTTOM) created by the art department were sent to the VAD, the Virtual Art Department (led by virtual environment supervisor Robert Powers) and built as digital 3-D objects (ABOVE, TOP LEFT and TOP RIGHT). These became part of a bank of thousands of digital assets used to populate the backgrounds of virtual sets. The helicoradians were originally inspired by the feathery feeding structures of the Christmas tree worm, a tube worm common on coral reefs. The big difference is scale: Christmas tree worms are only an inch or so across.

On February 21, 2007, performance capture in the Volume at Playa Vista in Los Angeles, CA, commenced. Performance capture carried on in earnest through the summer and into late October of that year, at which time the production team headed "down under" to New Zealand to begin the live-action shoot. In early March and through the summer, Playa Vista was used once again for some performance-capture pickups; the location remained a headquarters for production throughout.

ABOVE: Worthington on set at Playa Vista in late July 2007 during the "first sortie" scene in the forest and then the final render (OPPOSITE).

OVERLEAF: Frame grab of wood sprites gathering on and around Jake—a sign from Eywa—while Neytiri watches intently in the background.

OVERLEAF, INSET: Worthington performing this scene; note the rudimentary, hand-held "sticks," each bearing a "markered prop" of a wood sprite, which showed Worthington where they were, and when they were touching him, to create a realistic reaction.

To make the assembly of these proxy sets as quick and easy as possible, Cameron devised a grid system that consisted of numbered platforms on wheels, on which structures representing trees, branches, logs, hills, and so on, were mounted. For each scene, the stage crew could determine what combination of numbered platforms was required and quickly assemble those platforms accordingly, as if putting together a puzzle.

With the set assembled, Cameron blocked out camera coverage for the scene. Rather than take up time with the actors as he played around with shot compositions and camera movement—moving the virtual camera with digital characters and environments displayed on his monitor—Cameron roughed out each scene first with performance doubles who were with the production throughout. This "troupe" of half a dozen or so performers—stunt coordinator Garrett Warren, stunt doubles Alicia Vela-Bailey, Ilram Choi, and Reuben Langdon, and experienced performance capture actors Kevin Dorman, Woody Schultz, and Julene Renee—proved invaluable to the virtual-production process, enabling Cameron to gain some familiarity with the environments and characters in a scene.

The preshoot camera experimentation also cued the art department as to which parts of a digital environment were going to be emphasized in a shot. "If Jim was covering a scene from one side," said Matt Madden, "the art department didn't have to worry about the details of the environment on the other side. When it came time to shoot the actors, the virtual-art department had all the correct environment assets there." The art department was careful to pull *only* the assets that were absolutely required for a shot. The more digital assets, the more the increased data would slow down the system. "The environments were so rich and dense and detailed, anything they could do to narrow them down was very helpful." When all the assets had been gathered, Giant Studios conducted a test to ensure that real-time capture, as the shot was currently populated and dressed, was possible.

RIGHT: Neytiri approaches her father with Jake in tow, as the clan watches expectantly.

RIGHT, INSET: Here is the frame-accurate match of the original performance by Saldana. As was true for every CG-character in the film, every gesture and nuance of both body and facial performance were accurately preserved throughout the chain of shot development, until the final character is, and does, exactly what the actors did in the performance-capture sessions.

The same moment seen at three stages of production.

ABOVE: Frame grab from the finished shot of Neytiri defending Jake against Tsu'Tey. **OPPOSITE, TOP**: The same frame, as it appears in the intermediate "template" level. This is the "real time" model of Neytiri, in the Hometree interior virtual set, with kabuki face. The numbers at the top denote the focal length of the lens, and the information Weta will need to generate the shot in 3-D (meaning the interocular distance between the two virtual "eyes," as well as the convergence distance). The numbers below identify the capture take and the virtual camera take, and are used to track all the versions of the shot through the production system. **OPPOSITE, BOTTOM**: The same frame of action, from a reference camera, of Saldana as Neytiri during performance capture (early September 2007).

11.6mm i1.40 c208.1 167-750 090213T18

167_tk_X0A_002_Z1_pc010_0B07_VC_Av009_LE

"It was an ongoing struggle throughout the production to get the scenes to 'run,'" said Cameron. "As sets and lighting got more complex, and as more and more characters were added, more tricks and workarounds needed to be invented to get the scenes to run at a frame rate high enough to be considered 'real time.' It was a constant arms race between the continually rising complexity of the scenes and the ongoing development of new techniques to 'optimize' environments and characters, some of which were highly creative, such as breaking entire crowds down into moving two-dimensional 'cards' called zoetropes."

With digital-asset issues worked out beforehand, Cameron was able to concentrate solely on performance with the actors when they finally came onto the stage for the performance-capture work. "Jim spent almost all of his time on the floor working with the actors and getting the performances he wanted," noted Nolan Murtha. "He could focus all of his attention on the performers, knowing that if there was something in the camera work or staging of the scene he didn't like, he could change that down the road."

Without costumes, makeup, or the requirements of conventional photography to distract and slow them down, the actors, too, were able to focus on performance. One of the things Cameron had wanted to determine with

his original prototype scene was if actors would be comfortable with the virtual-production setup—wearing the head rigs and motion-capture suits—or if they would find it distracting. Both the prototype actors and, later, those working on the production responded very well to the setup. "We embraced the performance capture and had a lot of fun with it," Sam Worthington said. "Performance capture is incredibly freeing. You can't hide, so every take has to be truthful. At first it was a little nervewracking, but then you forget that you're wearing headgear and dots on your face." The filmmakers devised a number of ways to help the actors locate themselves emotionally on Pandora. If a scene included an explosion, they boomed a noise over amplifiers, threw foam particles and whacked the actors with jousting poles. To force the cast to walk carefully, as they would on Pandora's slick, mossy terrain, they laid giant plastic sheets on the ground.

Working with his actors in the performance-capture Volume, Cameron would most often begin by running them through preliminary blocking with the virtual camera in hand so that he could explore camera moves. Motion data from the actors was streamed into the command center of computers manned by Giant Studios. In real time, the performance capture was retargeted onto the

A leonopteryx mockup was made of foam and fiberglass, and mounted on a large gimbal. (**ABOVE, TOP**) Stunt rigger Mark Ginther pushes up the "leo's" nose as Jake and Neytiri climb upward out of the Tree of Souls caldera (mid-September 2007).

ABOVE, BOTTOM LEFT: Cameron and Worthington discuss how Jake will ride the leonopteryx.

ABOVE, BOTTOM RIGHT: A performance capture of Worthington shot from a slightly different angle—but of the same moment—as the frame grab from the final scene (**OPPOSITE**) of Jake landing.

OPPOSITE, TOP: Worthington during a training session led by stunt coordinator Garrett Warren.

OPPOSITE, BOTTOM: Two and a half months later at Playa Vista, Worthington (Jake) fights Alonso (Tsu'Tey); ABOVE, TOP: the monitor shows the performance as it is being captured; later, they switched to a knife fight.

ABOVE, BOTTOM: Cameron in the Volume working with the virtual camera during the fight sequence.

OPPOSITE: Saldana being captured riding on the banshee "gimbal rig." Worthington stands on a ladder nearby, in position for Saldana's eye-line, as if he is riding his banshee next to hers. The black robe, dubbed a "burka," prevents the motion-capture camera grid from "seeing" his markers. Each flyer had to be captured separately, since there was only one gimbal rig, and their motions were later combined into a single scene file. The stunt team tilts and banks the banshee mockup in perfect coordination with Saldana's athletic weight shifts. For safety, Saldana wears a body harness and is partially supported by cables, so if she falls off the gimbal, the stunt riggers can catch her before she hits the ground. An electric "ritter" fan hits Saldana with strong wind, so that she will feel, and account for, the movement of her hair. The color-coded "reference hair" is not picked up by the motion-capture system, but it influences the actors' performances and acts as a guide to the Weta animators. Cameron is tilting his outstretched arms to cue the stunt team to "bank left," as he watches video playback of a previously captured flight path. A few weeks later, banshee flight sessions continue (ABOVE, TOP and ABOVE, BOTTOM).

ABOVE, TOP: Cast members gather around Cameron as he explains the landing sequence of the leonopteryx into the Tree of Souls in the virtual environment. A month later, performance begins

ABOVE, BOTTOM: Saldana and Cameron share a laugh during a break in capture sessions.

video-game-resolution versions of the characters, moving within a low-res digital environment; that way, Cameron could see the scene played out with CG characters in a CG world on his monitor. Giant also streamed the low-res scene to the HD monitors onstage so that Cameron and the actors could see how the scene was playing in the digital world.

Any problems Cameron detected in his camera's digital view could be quickly adjusted by the virtual-art department, which was set up on its own area of the stage, in what the crew affectionately called "the lemonade stand." "That area of the stage was for what I called 'fixing an airplane in flight,'" said Robert Stromberg. "In the middle of shooting, if there was a problem, we could immediately address it and make the composition work by moving trees or rocks. It was like a little pit-crew area, where we could fix a set and put it back in the Volume so Jim could keep going. It was a way to keep production moving."

Weta Digital had developed real-time facial capture to be employed during the shoot, but production wound up not using it after the first few sessions. By using seventy or so rigid "blend shape" expressions, and morphing between them in real time—following a coarse mesh generated using the facial dots being shot by the head-rig

camera it was possible to have a real-time animated CG face, with moving lips and eyes. The point of the real-time setup was to enable Cameron to see how the actors' performances were translating to their CG characters, but the blend-shape expressions were too crude, and Cameron found them distracting.

Instead, the virtual production team just projected the actual video of the actor, shot by the head-rig camera, onto a smooth, featureless CG head. The technique, dubbed the "kabuki mask," had been used effectively in the prototype test. Cameron got the idea from the ghostly woman in the crystal ball at Disneyland's "Haunted Mansion," which was a riveting illusion accomplished by projecting a film of an actress onto a blank bust. Nolan Murtha's team figured out how to map the head-rig video onto a blank white mask, which was then attached to the CG character's head. The white mask was reminiscent of the makeup used in Japanese kabuki theater, and the name stuck, even though the process was later refined so that the face color matched the blue of the CG body.

The kabuki mask worked unexpectedly well in conveying the actor's performance. The actual eyes and mouth of the actor appeared, as video, on the CG character's face, which

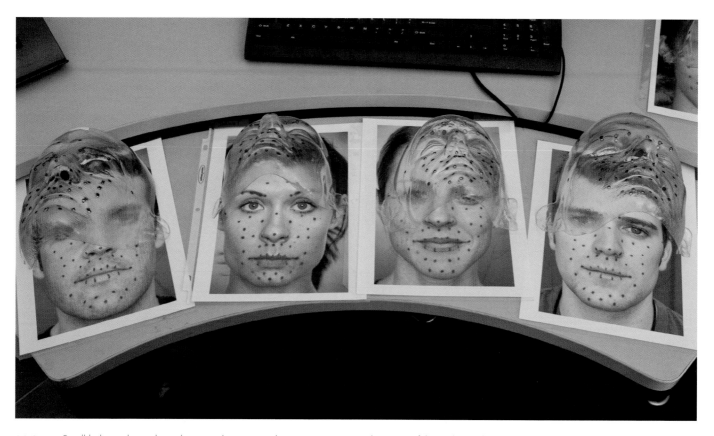

ABOVE: Small holes in these clear plastic masks were used to ensure consistent placement of the make-up dots. The dots were part of the image-based facial capture system, and were also used to align the head-rig cameras.

gave Cameron a much better sense of the performance, allowing him to select the takes he wanted to use in final shots. "It helped to communicate the emotional content of a performance," said Richie Baneham. "Not only was it an aid for Jim as a director and a camera operator, it also helped editorial to put together something that flowed emotionally."

After determining, in general terms, final blocking and how he would cover the scene, Cameron would typically put down the virtual camera and concentrate on the actors and their performances, recording them with a number of high-definition reference cameras. The purpose of these cameras was to capture clean reference of the actors' performances, without the fish-eye distortion produced by the head-rig camera. Though the head-rig camera provided the actual data that would drive image-based facial capture, the HD cameras provided reference that would help the Weta Digital animators to better understand the subtleties of the actors' performances.

Most importantly, the reference cameras were used by Cameron and the editors to select the best takes. They were the only watchable record of the performance at that stage of the game, since the head-rig camera produced a distorted image that was useless for editing performance, and the kabuki mask lacked enough detail to see subtleties in expression. In addition, the wider reference angles recorded hand and other body movement not picked up by the head-rig camera. The hand reference was especially critical, since the motion-capture system was able to record only rough approximations of hand movement. All the fine hand movement of the characters, including the contacts between hands and objects or surfaces, were created by the Weta animators by key-framing to match the reference images.

The reference angles were particularly effective since the HD cameras could be actually *in* the Volume with Cameron and the actors. In previous systems, reference cameras were banished to the sidelines of the Volume to avoid their blocking—or "occluding"—all or part of the actors from the motion-capture cameras.

But occlusion was less of an issue on *Avatar*, not only because facial capture was done with the head-rig camera rather than the motion-capture cameras, but also because of the power of Giant Studios' biomechanical solve to fill in occluded areas. With that superior performance-capture feature at his disposal, Cameron was able to have multiple HD cameras positioned all over the Volume, shooting

whatever angles he wanted. "We shot a *lot* of HD footage," noted Richard Baneham. "Sometimes we'd have as many as eight to twelve HD cameras on set at one time. We'd shoot a close-up, a medium, and a wide from complementary angles to the angle we were going to shoot the scene from. We had the HD operators lying on their backs on the ground, shooting up; we had them on ladders, shooting down. So we had the actor recorded from every distance and angle, which meant there was great reference for Weta."

"The rule of thumb was three reference cameras for a single character," said Cameron. "One for the close-up, one for a medium shot that included the hands, and one for a wide shot of the entire body. Two actors in a scene would typically require four cameras—a dedicated close-up for each, and the medium and wide coverage shared by common cameras. This principle was extrapolated through larger numbers of people, up to a maximum of twelve reference cameras. But every actor always got a dedicated close-up camera. Where it got complicated was when actors had several different positions during a single scene, requiring multiple dedicated close-up cameras for a single character as they turned from one position to another. Often it was necessary to break a scene in the middle, so the reference cameras could be reset for close-ups after the actors changed positions. Sometimes it was necessary to capture a few of the characters in a scene separately, because the crew ran out of cameras. These separate 'passes' could get quite complex, technically, in the matching of sync and position."

The HD cameras were also instrumental in guiding the actors' performances. On previous motion-capture projects, actors performed only for the distant, ceiling-mounted motion-capture cameras within a large, empty Volume. As a result, the actors had no sense of when they were in close-up or in a wide shot—every shot felt the same on the motion-capture stage, regardless of how it would ultimately be composed in the final CG scene. That tended to make for generic, rather than shot-specific, performances. "Actors act differently depending on the camera," said Glenn Derry. "If you're doing a wide master of a scene, they are going to be a little more grand in their motion than they would be in a close-up. If the talent doesn't know when they are in a close-up or when they are in a wide shot, you lose all those subtle differences in their performance, and the performance is not as good."

With the HD cameras in the Volume with them, the actors had an idea of how Cameron was going to shoot their scene, and they could adjust their performances accordingly. "If a character was going to be in close-up," said Matt Madden, "Jim would tell the HD operator to frame it that way. So the actor would see that HD camera right there shooting him in close-up, even though there was simultaneous coverage going on with the other HD cameras, too. That didn't mean Jim wouldn't go back later and do a different angle, but the actors understood how to play the shot when they were there on the stage. They could physically see where the live-action cameras were as they were performing."

Also in the Volume, along with the performers and the HD cameras, were whatever crude set pieces or props were needed for realistic interaction between the performers and their environment. In some cases, the scale of that interaction was just too large to simulate onstage. The destruction

ABOVE: Actor Wes Studi (Eytukan, leader of the Omaticaya clan) speaking during a performance-capture session. Note the bank of six reference cameras shooting the performances; each is assigned a different character. The reference images were absolutely critical, both for the editors to choose the best takes during performance editing, and for the Weta animators to check that the nuances of the actors' performances were coming through the facial capture system. There would sometimes be up to twelve reference cameras in the Volume, shooting close-ups, medium shots, and wide angles of all the main characters in the scene. This image also shows the relatively featureless shooting environment—the "black box" theater style in which the performance-capture scenes were shot.

of Hometree, in which the massive tree falls and hundreds of displaced, frightened Na'vi scramble out of the way, was one such scene. Previsualization supervisor Brad Alexander and his crew created 3-D animations of the falling tree. That animation was then loaded into the onstage motion-capture system so that Cameron could see the action in real time in his virtual-camera monitor as he directed the actors to flee.

Precanned sound effects loaded into a synthesizer onstage and broadcast through a PA system also enhanced actor interaction with the Hometree destruction. Working the soundboard, Cameron cranked up thunderous booms to simulate the sound of the tree crashing to the ground and to create a sense of fear and panic, and also approximate timings, for the actors. Canned sounds of helicopter rotors and creature roars served the same purpose for other scenes. Sometimes the sound effects were live rather than canned. For the scene in which Neytiri has to kill a wounded viperwolf, for example, assistant director Josh McLaglen stood in for the viperwolf, lying on the floor and making pathetic crying, yelping sounds. The cries were so convincing, Cameron left them as an element in the final sound mix for the scene.

After the performance-capture sessions with the actors, Cameron would do a rough cut of the scene, choosing specific takes from the HD video reference with coeditors Stephen Rivkin and John Refoua. "Because he'd blocked out those HD cameras very closely to how he was going to ultimately cover the scene," said Matt Madden, "he could do a rough cut based on the HD video."

"The reference cameras were our bible in terms of what the actual performances were," said Stephen Rivkin. "When we cut our performance edit, we would look at nothing but people in black suits with dots, and that would remain in our edit, underneath all of the other virtual cameras, so that we could always refer back to them."

Once the scene had been cut using the HD recordings of the actors in their suits and head rigs, all of the virtual-production departments would receive this cut version of the scene so that they could prepare for a final virtual-camera session. "The rough cut told us exactly what characters and environments were going to be needed for the camera session," said Matt Madden. "We'd make sure all the motion was refined, all the sets were tweaked, and everything was ready to run in real time."

OPPOSITE: Neytiri and the clan in the midst of the chaos; (OPPOSITE, INSET) on set, falling debris was mimicked by small foam props tossed in the air around the actors.

ABOVE, TOP: The devastating scene of Hometree falling.

ABOVE, BOTTOM: Concept painting by Cole.

After rebuilding the CG scene with more refined motion, the team would sit down with Cameron to review it, still in low-resolution form. At this review session, Cameron would ask for environment or lighting changes, or change the timing of a piece of action, or add atmospheric effects. "We were able to adjust those things very quickly," said Nolan Murtha, "because we were still working with low-resolution assets. We could swap out a whole environment very quickly if we had to, or change a scene from night to day, or add whatever effects Jim wanted—all in a very short amount of time."

Each performance take of this revised CG scene was dubbed a "camera load," indicating its readiness for a final virtual-camera session. "The scene would be loaded into the virtual camera," said Murtha, "and Jim would go back out to the Volume by himself, and do shots. We would replay the motion over and over again; he would see it as a low-res scene on his monitor and do whatever he needed with the camera to get his shot." These camera sessions sometimes took place just days after the original performance capture, but usually they took place months later.

The camera sessions were the heart of the *Avatar* virtual production process. This was the moment of maximum visual creativity. The emotional creativity had been done months earlier with the actors; now it was time for the lighting and the camera movement to turn theater into cinema. Cameron personally operated the virtual camera during these sessions, just as he would operate the 3-D camera during the live-action shoot in Wellington, New Zealand, on all but the Steadicam shots. This lent a stylistic continuity to the camera moves, since the same compositional eye and operating style were in both places. It was hoped that this would help create a seamless blend of the live-action and CG realms.

Unlike on the live-action stage, however, the virtual camera and the actors were not required to be together in one place, at one time. In fact, given the small but annoying lag through the virtual camera system, it was difficult to follow fast action when the scene was being captured live. It was found preferable to capture the scene, prepare it with all its motion edits and environment tweaks, and then shoot all the camera coverage later, with complete control. Usually, in order to obviate the effects of the lag, the virtual scene was played back at half speed or even slower, so that Cameron could follow the action. Half speed was the slowest practical speed for dialogue scenes; any slower and the dialogue dur-

ing playback sounded too distorted to follow. A good camera operator takes cues from the dialogue, so hearing what the actors were saying was critical to "feeling" the scene.

Cameron felt that the camera should flow instinctively, based on the drama of the moment. Shooting with the virtual camera required the entire physicality of the operator, turning the cameraman's body into whatever platform was needed, from dolly to crane, to helicopter. By changing the scale of the scene relative to the operator's physical size in the Volume, the handheld camera could be made to soar through many multiples of the cameraman's physical reach. One-to-one was used for close coverage of the characters. Three-to-one would turn a two-foot raise of the operator's arms into a six-foot jib-arm move, equivalent to a small camera crane. Five-to-one, and a three-foot rise became fifteen feet, now equal to a larger crane, such as a Supertechno. A ratio of fifty-to-one was the equivalent of a camera mounted on a helicopter. The freedom was complete. The very same performance take, done once by the actor months earlier, could now be shot in any manner desired, from an extreme close-up to a sweeping helicopter shot. And coverage of this one performance take, from several different camera angles, could all be cut together with seamless continuity.

Cameron would operate the virtual camera in the empty Volume, the lights dimmed to improve viewing of the monitor, alone except for an assistant who wrangled the camera's umbilical cable. The shooting days were long, sometimes sixteen or eighteen hours, and often Cameron could be seen stretching to relieve the pain in his back from supporting the camera. While shooting, he would move with total focus, sliding his feet across the floor while conserving balance as in tai chi. Performed by hand, the camera had an organic connection to the moving subject, but some of the jittery handheld motion would need to be smoothed out, without losing the "life" in the move. "A number of smoothing algorithms were created," said Cameron, "and assigned different numbers, which would correspond to different real-world camera platforms. A Number One would only remove the high-frequency jitter, while retaining a 'handheld' quality. A Two would be more like a Steadicam, smoother but still organic. A Three would give the smoothness of dolly track, or a camera crane." Cameron would do a take, then ask the stage operator, at his workstation nearby, to "save it, and give me a Number Three smooth." After a couple of minutes of rendering, the shot would be displayed for approval. If it was good, it would go right into the Avid, for the editor, who was also working nearby, to cut into the scene.

The virtual process allowed the exploration of any camera move and any creative impulse. The beauty of the virtual system was that during playback, the characters always did exactly the same thing on every take, so it was possible to refine a camera move over multiple tries. "Often in live action," Cameron commented, "the camera and lighting would be perfect, but not the performance, or vice versa. The virtual camera allowed the best camera move and lighting to coincide with the actor's best take."

Once final camera movements had been added to the low-res scene, it would be edited to its precise length and sent to the virtual lab for refinement. Cameron would describe any changes he wanted—more smoke, for example, or an adjustment in the lighting—and the lab would make those changes. Concurrently, the 3-D crew would set the interocular and convergence parameters in the scene. The final, refined scene, called the "template," was then sent to Weta, informing the artists there exactly how the camera should move in their finals; which takes of the performances should be used; and the layout of the environment, down to the smallest blade of grass. It was, in essence, a 3-D-video-game version of the final scene as it would appear in the film. "Everything that was going to be in the final image was there in this video-game-resolution version," said Murtha.

The production team also supplied Weta with performance-captured stunts and action material. Though the actors had been trained to perform many of their own stunts, the troupe of production stunt performers stood in for them in the more demanding physical scenes, such as the one in which Jake and the Na'vi hunters climb long vines stretched between floating boulders to make their way to the mountaintop banshee rookery. Production created a special vertical Volume for the scene to give the performers adequate climbing heights. To suggest the agility and prowess of the Na'vi warriors, Cameron performance-captured the stunt performers attached to cables, which helped lift them up set pieces representing the rocks. Weta animators had to tweak the performance capture, which lacked some of the weight and dynamics of characters actually pulling themselves

OPPOSITE: Cameron creating a shot, September 2007.

upward, and also adjusted foot and hand placements to improve the contact points between the CG characters and the rocky surfaces, but the cable-assisted performance capture provided the basic action for the climb.

Stunt performers also doubled for creatures in special performance-capture sessions intended to work out basic blocking and timings. "It was in no way indicative of the final creature animation," said Richard Baneham, "but it told us what kind of moves were being done, when the character was moving right to left. Weta would then take it to the next level, animating the creature fully and sending it back to us in a low-res form so we could shoot cameras on it."

Having the creature action drive the camera was a far better approach than the way CG creatures are usually dealt with in films. Typically, live-action plates for such scenes are shot first, and then the animators have to fit their CG creature into the space and time given them in the preexisting shot. Often, it is a tight or awkward fit.

In contrast, *Avatar*'s shots were composed around a creature's action, as if the thanator or viperwolf had been on location, visible in the director's viewfinder as he moved his camera to keep the animal in the frame. "Because of that," said Baneham, "there is an energy to the scenes that feels like live action. The camera is truly alive."

In one performance-captured creature scene, stunt performer Nito Larioza moved on all fours to portray a viperwolf's physical interaction with Jake. "With Nito's performance," said Baneham, "we could have him knock down Sam Worthington, and then, when the animators had to replace Nito with an actual animated viperwolf, the weight was there. We knew where the viperwolf was in space at every point in the scene, and we knew all the weight transfers. Obviously, we weren't married to Nito's performance, but we had all the interaction between him and the other actor, and that lent credibility to the creature."

The stunt crew also performed viperwolf action for the scene in which the entire pack advances on Jake and then chases him through the forest. To block out the basic action and determine spatial relationships, they carried weighted gym bags—with calibrators attached that made them visible as viperwolves in the virtual camera—and chased Sam Worthington through the set. "That became a blocking and choreography reference for where the viperwolves would be and how they would hunt as a pack and interact not only with Sam, but with one another," said Baneham. "We held the bags a little over knee height, which gave us the right

level and also helped the actors with eye-lines, so they could understand where the dogs were at what point. It was a very crude method, but the eye-lines of the performers were much truer because of it, and the animators were better able to understand what the intention of the blocking was, and then they could concentrate on creating high-quality animation and spend their time where it was really warranted."

Among the most complex aspects of the creature-related capture was realizing characters atop their flying banshees—an important part of Na'vi culture, and a critical element of the narrative. Finding the method to integrate the riders to the banshees proved to be one of the most difficult tasks in the capture phase of the production. Early on the idea favored by the effects experts was to use a motion-base to simulate the banshee's movement. It would be programmed with pitch, yaw, and roll moves according to the pre-captured flight paths, and then the actors would be captured riding it.

Cameron rejected that idea, noting that the riders were supposed to be in control of their mounts, not the other way around. On a motion-base they would just be along for the ride, rather than initiating the various flight maneuvers. So the crew devised a manually operated gimbal rig that could move freely on multiple axes and that would respond to the actor's weight shifts, just as a real banshee would. To create the organic interplay between beast and rider, the rig was moved manually by several stuntmen, as well as taking the physical inputs from the rider's change in position. This sounded good in theory, and looked promising initially, but a number of harsh realities quickly emerged.

For example, it was assumed that the rider would lean his weight in the direction of a turn, as one would on a motorcycle. But in early tests with an acrobatically trained stunt woman, this proved disastrous, because a winged creature, like an airplane, banks as it turns. By leaning in the direction of the banked turn, the rider wound up tipping even more downhill, and would fall right out of the saddle. So although it was counterintuitive, the opposite approach was tried. The stunt players would lean away from the direction of the turn, shifting their weight "uphill" as the creature banked. The riders flexed their legs to shift their weight upward, which served to keep the rider level, and with their center of mass over the centerline of the banshee. This immediately looked better and made more visual sense.

Cameron was seeking an athletic, jockey-like riding style for the Na'vi, something more akin to a board sport, like surfing or snowboarding, than to sitting passively in the saddle of a horse. So the stunt performers were asked to ride balanced on foot pegs, similar to the pegs of a dirt bike, with their weight carried fully by their thigh muscles. The performers quickly found the posture produced agonized quad muscles the next day. Flying in the jockey pose was soon dubbed the "Banshee Buns-of-Steel Workout." To avoid cramping, the actors donned seat-harnesses and were connected to wires that took some but not all of their weight. This also provided a margin of safety. In case the performer fell off the gimbal rig, the stunt riggers could catch them by taking all their weight on the wires before they hit the floor. Neville Page in the creature department was called upon to redesign the clavicles and breathing intakes of the banshee, to create the necessary purchase for the Na'vi feet as they ride. A banshee saddle was designed, complete with wood and bone riding pegs that clamped to the banshee's anatomy, with straps that locked the assembly to the banshee without restricting the movement of the wings. The banshee had to be ridden bareback, when Jake first captures one, or with a saddle, as the experienced Na'vi riders do, and the changes to the anatomy allowed for both possibilities.

After months of testing, the dynamic riding style of the Na'vi was worked out, ready for the actors to try. Saldana and Worthington embraced the physical challenge of riding the creatures, knowing that riding was such an important part of their characters. They quickly learned to balance and shift their weight with powerful positive thrusts, equal to the muscular power of the beast they were riding, and to act with full emotion while performing complex maneuvers. All of this took practice, practice, practice. Jake learns to fly during the course of the story, but Neytiri is already an "ace pilot" by the time we first meet her, so Saldana had to ramp up to expert level very quickly. Her martial arts training and horseback riding now paid off, as those months of muscle conditioning enabled her to create a dynamic physical performance equal to her powerful character. She soon was able to make flying a banshee look effortless, graceful, and exhilarating, which was vital to the dreamlike wish-fulfillment aspect of the storytelling.

"Jake eventually becomes an expert himself," noted Cameron, "so even though Sam could initially use the awkwardness of learning to balance on the gimbal rig as part of his performance, he eventually needed to master the same grace and power as Zoë. Not only did he achieve that, and prove it in the scene where they fly together,

ABOVE: Back at Playa Vista in late April 2009, Baneham, Landau, and Cameron review footage with lead virtual stage operator Dan Fowler as well as Vince Pace and VFX supervisor Steven Quale.

zigzagging through the forest canopy while chased by the leonopteryx, but Sam went beyond the banshee riding techniques to create his own unique riding style when it came time to ride the leonopteryx." This enormous beast, huge even for a Na'vi, could not be ridden like a banshee, because its size and structure prevented the same foot supports that the banshee offered. In addition, Cameron was looking for something special, a style befitting the mythic leader, Toruk Macto, "The Rider of Last Shadow."

A much larger gimbal rig was created for the leonopteryx, following the same principles as the banshee rig. Worthington and his stunt double Reuben Langdon began experimenting with techniques for riding the broad back of the creature. Worthington called upon his years as an expert surfer to come up with a dynamically balanced stance that allowed him to shift his weight during highly banked turns, and still be able to fire the .30-caliber machine gun that Jake carries in battle. He came up with a vocabulary of movement that looked athletic and powerful, a style one would expect of a mighty warrior king.

The last step to all of this flight capture was to integrate the motion of the riders to the movement of the creatures, in sync with the flight paths captured by Cameron and Baneham months earlier. Since motion control was not being used, all the gimbal movement was done according to verbal cues, based on a visual playback of the previous flight path capture. Baneham would stand in front of a monitor and signal the banking cues to the rider and the gimbal operators, by literally moving his outspread arms in sync with the creature on the screen and yelling "bank left." The verbal cues had to be bellowed over the sound of a huge electric "ritter" wind machine, which Cameron insisted on using so the actors would account for the way their hair was blown across their face when they turned their heads to look behind. "It was all crude, crazily exhilarating, and it worked," said Cameron. "It preserved the organic interaction of rider and banshee."

Later, the rider's motion was refined with motion editing to be in perfect sync with the banshee, and the separately captured riders were added together, to create pairs and groups of flying creatures, as the scenes required. Terry Notary, the movement expert, was even called upon to create wing flaps for the creatures. A special CG banshee was rigged to take input from a human performer, and Notary acted out wing flaps in sync with the previously captured flight path moves. This allowed the team in Playa Vista to intuitively create the banshee flight dynamics, with small flaps to sustain lift, gliding pauses, and deep power strokes when the creature was climbing or fleeing from attack.

ABOVE: Cameron and Saldana during the Hometree eyrie scene in which Jake meets Neytiri's banshee, Tse'zey, for the first time. Cameron is puppeteering the action of the foam prop of Tse'zey's mouth opening and closing, which gave Saldana a sense of the banshee as a real character in the scene (May 2007). The performance-capture session matches the frame grab (OPPOSITE, BOTTOM) in time but not in point of view; the camera angle for the session at Playa Vista is a still from an HD reference camera side view of the action; the angle in the frame grab was chosen by Cameron at a later point.

When it was all put together, and then shot by Cameron using the virtual camera, it provided a surprisingly complete and compelling template from which the Weta animators would work. The Weta team would later provide all the subtle nuances that brought creatures and riders to life—the blowing hair, the flexing of the riders' legs in time with the creatures' wing flaps, the high-frequency fluttering of the trailing edges of the wing membranes during gliding flight, the whipping of the tail during high-performance banks, or the quick turn of the animal's head as its "chin vane" acted as a control surface to initiate a turn. All of these tiny details combined to make a dream-like fantasy come fully alive.

The first sixty-two days of production, which took place from January well into March 2007, were all-consuming, sixteen-hour days for the filmmakers. Long days of shooting and problem solving would continue for another seven months, but the pressure let up ever so slightly as Cameron and his crew gained proficiency in the innovative production techniques. Finally, by October 2007, the bulk of the performance-capture material had been shot. There would be pickups in the last year of production, but, for now, the performance-capture stage in Playa Vista went quiet, as Cameron and his crew traveled halfway around the world to shoot *Avatar*'s live action.

ABOVE: Stunt performer Reuben Langdon enacts the movement of his backpack being snatched in the thanator's jaws in the Volume at Playa Vista.

PREVIOUS SPREAD: Neytiri perched atop a tree branch, silently stalking Jake's avatar (frame grab).

PREVIOUS SPREAD, INSET: Saldana performing the scene, perched on a riser in the Volume at Playa Vista.

ABOVE, TOP LEFT: Cameron talks Weaver through the scene. In the barren Volume, his descriptions helped the actors imagine the environment around them (late July 2007). ABOVE, TOP RIGHT: Weaver plays Grace in the Volume at Playa Vista. She is inside a "non-occluding" mesh mockup of the Samson, suspended on wires to simulate the motion of the vehicle. This allowed her to react naturally to the banking and shuddering of the ship as they fly a search pattern, as her character looks for Jake before the sun goes down. Her gyro-stabilized binoculars are represented by a simplified motion-capture prop. All the props and set pieces used in the Volume—large and small—were tagged. The tags helped match physical props to the objects they represented in the virtual world.

ABOVE, BOTTOM: A frame grab of the finished scene.

OPPOSITE: The Samson flying through the floating mountains of Pandora (frame grab).

While the "prototype" test of this scene was made in late 2005 with other actors, the performance-capture images, shown on this spread, depict the actual scene as it was captured nearly a year and a half later with Worthington.

OPPOSITE: An early study of the Pandoran jungle at night, with bioluminescence; this painting was later refined by Cole to more closely match the final color palette.

ABOVE, TOP: Frame grab of Jake fending off the viperwolf pack.

ABOVE, BOTTOM LEFT: Match-frame of Worthington during the performance-capture session for the image above. Josh McLaglen runs past in the background carrying a stunt pad representing a viperwolf—part of a pack of stuntmen circling Worthington on set.

ABOVE, BOTTOM RIGHT: Baneham and stunt performers block out the viperwolf action for the scene.

ABOVE: Actress CCH Pounder (Mo'at) reaching to connect with a strand of the Tree of Souls—and Eywa—in the Volume, the last day of August 2007.

OPPOSITE: The Tree of Souls at night. Originally much brighter, the floor underwent significant design exploration; various root systems and different-scaled proportions of the well area were explored. In this "closer-to-final" painting, Cole reduced the iridescent glow of the floor, and Cameron then drew in a pattern that suggested a network radiating from the tree's lower trunk.

ABOVE, TOP: Worthington and Cameron became good friends over the long course of the production (mid-September 2007). ABOVE, BOTTOM: Between takes at Playa Vista, Worthington and Lang—being introduced by Cameron—meet for the first time while Landau (far left) and Stan Winston Studio effects supervisor John Rosengrant look on (mid-September 2007). OPPOSITE: Jake's wrists are bound as the clan discovers his double-dealing with Quaritch; they are, as yet, unaware that he has had a change of heart (performance-capture session, early August 2007).

The "Tree of Voices" glade was based on willow trees and Japanese gardens, to create an idyllic and romantic setting, like an alien version of a Maxfield Parrish painting. For those in the Volume on this day (late April 2007), the feeling of excitement was said to have been "magical," "palpable." Ethereal electronic music was played over a PA system to create the mood as Worthington and Saldana entered the mystical glade.

ABOVE, BOTTOM LEFT: Cameron talks to Worthington and Saldana about the timing of the kiss. Later, during the actual take, Cameron—along with Stephen Rosenbaum (seen in the lower-left corner)—watch closely on the reference cameras during the kiss (ABOVE, TOP). During playback, Saldana used the images of the virtual set on the monitors to imagine the willow glade around her (ABOVE, BOTTOM RIGHT). Note for this scene Rosenbaum opted to remove the head rigs, which interfered with the kiss itself. Instead, a bank of HD reference cameras shot close-ups of the actors' faces, and Weta animators would later use key-frame techniques to recreate every nuance of the actors' expressions "the old-fashioned way."

OPPOSITE, TOP: A frame grab from the final scene and the corresponding moment from performance-capture (OPPOSITE, BOTTOM).

OPPOSITE: Worthington's performance (OPPOSITE, TOP) and the final render of the same scene (OPPOSITE, BOTTOM).

ABOVE: CCH Pounder as Mo'at assessing the outsider (Jake) her daughter has brought back to Hometree. The template is shown here (ABOVE, BOTTOM), as well as the performance-capture still (pulled from an HD reference camera at an alternate angle) (ABOVE, INSET) of the exact same performance; this footage is also precisely what was used to build the frame grab seen here (ABOVE, TOP). Note that the natural-looking firelight created by Weta Digital is quite different from the lighting generated by the bioluminescent patterning of Mo'at's face, which are embedded within the skin of the Na'vi.

ABOVE and OPPOSITE: In the Rookery, a wild banshee roars at Jake as he approaches; Jake roars back (frame grabs).

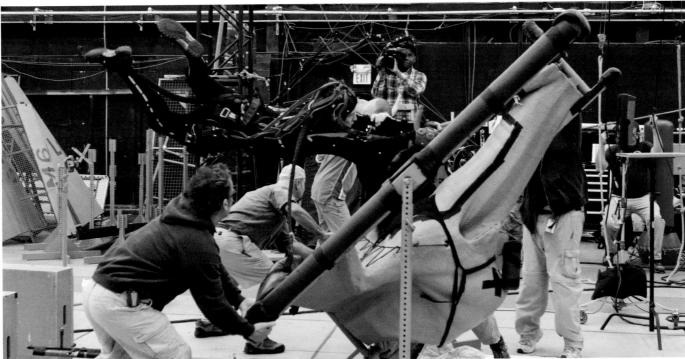

ABOVE, TOP: Cameron and Worthington sharing a laugh between takes.

ABOVE, BOTTOM: Worthington on a full-tilt banshee ride in the Volume (June 2007).

OPPOSITE, TOP: Cameron evaluating Neytiri's landing at the Rookery (early May 2007).

OPPOSITE, BOTTOM: Cameron and Worthington reviewing a playback of the virtual camera, during a banshee-flying session on stage at Playa Vista (late May 2007).

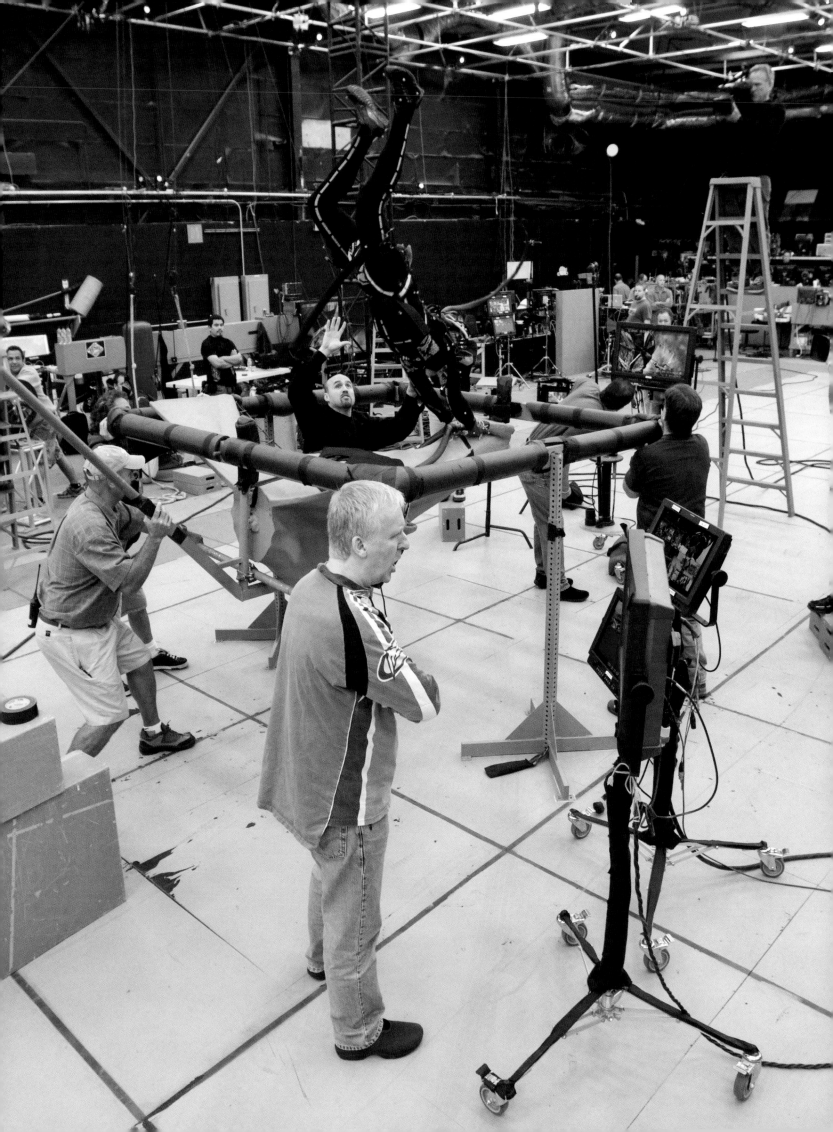

Garret Warren spots Worthington as cables pull the actor up, simulating the violent effect the diving wild banshee has on Jake. In the foreground, Cameron calls the cues, watching a playback of a previously captured flight path for timing (**LEFT**); Worthington holds on tight as cables yank him around (**OPPOSITE**).

BELOW: Jake's avatar on his first ride, struggling for control of his new banshee (frame grab).

ABOVE, TOP and OPPOSITE, TOP: Neytiri and Jake flying together; both of these photographs represent individual performance-capture sessions; both stills are the first layer upon which Weta then built the template. The template is then turned into the final render, seen here in both frame grabs (ABOVE, BOTTOM and OPPOSITE, BOTTOM).

OVERLEAF: Neytiri and Jake bank past the arched rock formations surrounding the Tree of Souls, at sunset (frame grab). These arches formed when iron crystals were deposited along the flux lines of the powerful magnetic fields of the Flux Vortex, and then over subsequent eons the surrounding rock eroded away.

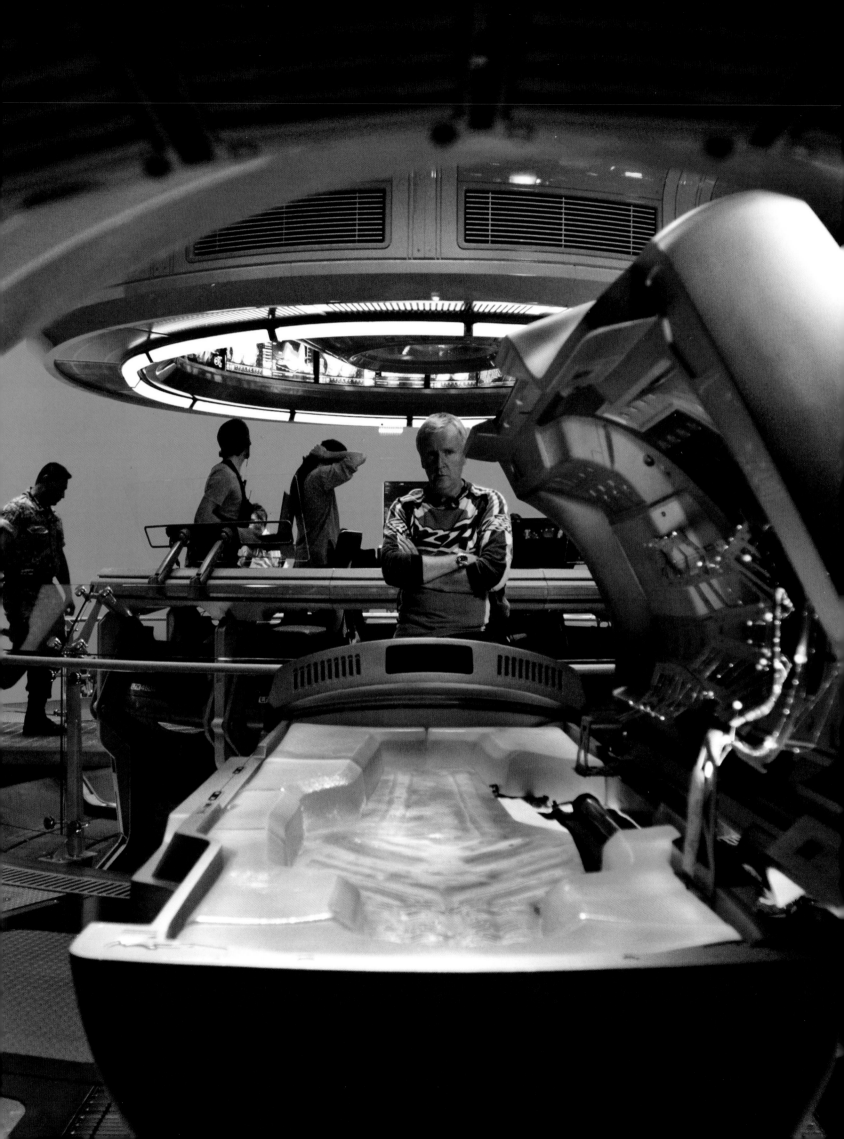

Cameron. Once in L.A., Taylor was treated to a tour of the Lightstorm art department, where he saw the maquettes, paintings, and drawings done by the concept artists up to that point. "It was all very stimulating and rather mind-boggling," said Taylor. "It completely floored me. I don't think I had ever seen anything so spectacular. The design team had been printing their illustrations out on these massive printers, so there were conceptual paintings as big as a huge oil painting mounted on the walls. Just walking into that environment was incredibly inspirational."

Cameron's passionate descriptions of the Na'vi and the world of Pandora, too, were inspirational, and Taylor returned home from the meeting very charged up about *Avatar.* "My only concern, initially," said Taylor, "was that all the work had been done. Was there anything we could add to that? I was concerned that the world may have already been fleshed out to such a degree that there would be very strong restraints put on our work. But that was not at all the case. There was a complete freedom to develop this culture around the parameters already established."

With Taylor's commitment to the film, Cameron and Landau expected that the first thing that would come out of Weta Workshop would be prop designs; instead, Taylor and his Workshop crew first presented *ideas*—ideas about Na'vi social structure, their cultural reference points, their lineage, and their religion. "The reason we felt the need to do that," said Taylor, "is that you can't determine whether a character in a film should carry a hunting bow if they're vegetarian. You don't put them in a waterproof environment if it doesn't rain in this forest. There was a need to flesh out the people and their world and culture before we could actually design the specifics."

Central to the development of Na'vi culture was an understanding of their religion. Based on the screenplay, Workshop members imagined a hierarchal, nature-based belief system that would be expressed in the way the Na'vi hunted, the way they viewed their kills, and the way they communicated. When the key cultural and societal questions had been answered, Weta Workshop began to design Na'vi weapons, living quarters, and clothing, building samples even of those items that would only be created in CG. "Jim and Rick Carter both felt very strongly from the beginning that if we were going to communicate the subtleties of the textures, the weaving styles, the translucency of the jewelry, the vicious edge on the side of a weapon, it needed to be created for real," said Taylor. "It needed to exist as a physical prop that the director, the art department. and the digital-effects facility could handle and touch."

Na'vi clothing, of course, would only be seen in CG, but Weta Workshop designed Na'vi garments with all the care of those that would be sewn and worn by a live actor. Workshop artists made sample pieces, finding inspiration in New Zealand's native Maori culture, known for its beautiful, intricate weaving. A young New Zealand fashion designer/costumer named Claire Prebble, who had twice won first place in the World of Wearable Art's annual exhibition, worked with Weta Workshop to create intricate weaves and beading for the Na'vi clothing. Later, Prebble flew to Los Angeles and continued to play an important role in the fine detailing of many memorable Na'vi costumes, including Mo'at's dramatic white ceremonial gown.

"We were able to draw on amazing talent in the generating of these pieces of clothing and this incredibly fine jewelry and props that the Na'vi use," said Taylor. The form of Na'vi clothing followed its function, which was, primarily, to allow for comfort and ease of movement in a hot, humid, and dense tropical forest. That main criterion was met by dressing the Na'vi scantily, with heavier ornamental pieces added for ceremonial purposes.

Weta Workshop drew on the flora and fauna of Pandora, as illustrated in concept art, to create textures for the clothing and props. "There are thorns that when embellished and set into another piece of construction become a formidable weapon," said Taylor. "Sap milked out of the branches of a tree has a crystalline quality that could be tooled into beautiful jewelry." Weta Workshop fabricated many such organic textures and pieces using state-of-the-art 3-D printing and laser-cutting technology, and incorporated them into the costume samples.

Many indigenous cultures were studied for their clothing and ornamentation. "It was observed by the design team that most indigenous people do not share our 'civilized' sense of shame about our bodies," Cameron commented, "and may wear elaborate ornamental clothing that hides little of what we would tend to cover." Extrapolating from that idea, the Na'vi clothing is minimal, but they wear complex ornamental necklaces, mantles, and headpieces. Cameron was insistent that the tops worn by female characters never look like "bikini tops" whose primary purpose was hiding the breasts. As a concession to the PG-13 rating, it was necessary to limit the exposure of Na'vi breasts, but it was important that the designs look

FOUR

KEM: ACTION

In October 2007, *Avatar*'s production crew moved to Stone Street Studios, near Peter Jackson's Weta production complex in Wellington, New Zealand. Prior to starting preproduction on *Avatar*, James Cameron had befriended Jackson and had listened, intrigued, as the director described the vibrant filmmaking community in Wellington. Later, Cameron and Landau toured the studios and, impressed, made the decision—early on—to establish the facility as *Avatar*'s base for live-action filming. Not only would it provide state-of-the-art production facilities, but shooting there would put Cameron in proximity to the team at Weta Digital just as they were moving into heavy creative and technical development, making him readily available for conferences and reviews of animation and related CG tests.

Shooting there would also give Cameron access to Weta Workshop, the venerated facility—founded by Richard Taylor and Tania Rodgers—that had been responsible for designing and building the physical aspects of Tolkien's Middle-earth for the *Lord of the Rings* films. By the time production arrived on the scene for the live-action shoot, Weta Workshop had been working on *Avatar* for a full year, creating a variety of setpieces and props to represent the diverse cultures of the Na'vi and the RDA teams.

Weta Workshop's involvement had begun with a phone call from Jon Landau to Richard Taylor, asking if he would come to Los Angeles to meet with

OPPOSITE: Cameron standing over a Link Unit in the newly finished link room set at the Stone Street Studios, in Wellington, New Zealand (mid-December 2007).

like they only incidentally covered the nipples, as if that was not their primary function.

Some of the early Weta Workshop designs, such as the Na'vi bows and knives, and some of the woven or beaded costume pieces, were incorporated directly into the film, whereas other costumes went through many permutations back in Los Angeles, in later months. Mayes Rubio, who had done the memorable Mayan costumes and jewelry for *Apocalypto*, was hired as costume designer to pull all the concepts together into one definitive culture. Some of the Weta Workshop sketches were fabricated by her team in Los Angeles, with frequent fittings on tall, lithe models for presentation to Cameron. Later, when Rubio moved on to another production, Debra Scott, who had won an Academy Award for her designs on *Titanic*, was asked to take over as costume designer. Scott returned to some of the Weta Workshop designs, and elaborated on them with her own renderings. Again, each and every costume was created physically by Debra's team before it was built in CG. This assured that all colors and textures would be accurate and look real to the eye, even though they would ultimately be seen only as computer models.

Soon after Weta Workshop had started on the Na'vi costume designs, the filmmakers expanded the team's assignment to include designing and building military props such as flak jackets and breathing masks for the Hell's Gate personnel—all pieces that, unlike the Na'vi accouterments, would have to be fabricated in quantity to service the live-action shoot.

Cameron, due to his long experience as a diver, had very specific ideas about the breathing masks in particular, and Workshop artists extrapolated on those ideas in building the final masks. "There are military versions and civilian versions and medical versions of the masks," said Taylor. "They required some very clever two-part injection-molding technology. Anything that touched the actor's face on the inside was soft and flexible, and then, on the outside, there was a rigid urethane material to hold the glass at the front of the mask." To pump clean air into the mask, Weta Workshop installed small fans in the backpacks worn by the characters, supposedly the source of battery power for the breathing masks. "Inside those were the little fans that pumped clean air up into the actors' noses." Later, because the facemasks reflected all the lights on the set, it was decided that the glass would be removed from the masks and added later using CG.

Weta Workshop built all the guns for the film, as well, suggesting a futuristic, but not *too* futuristic, technology. One gun was designed as a modular piece that could be transformed from a submachine gun into a rocket launcher. "We wanted to convey the idea that the use of steel has become limited in this world," said Taylor, "creating a need for modular components. So we created these modular systems where, in theory, all of these gun components would clip together." The Workshop built ammunition shells for the guns that were square rather than cylindrical, to give them a futuristic feeling, while retaining the visceral power of flying brass casings during the combat scenes.

ABOVE: Cameron and Richard Taylor review a mock-up of the Hydra 50-caliber machine gun (shortly after the Hawaii trip at Weta Workshop, February 2007).

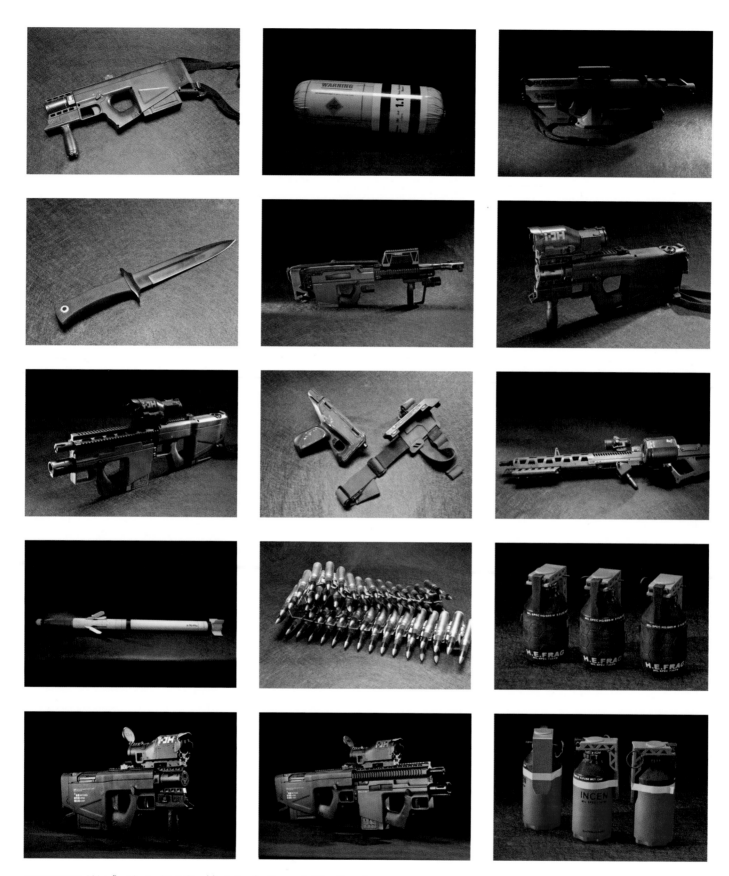

OPPOSITE: Wainfleet (actor Matt Gerald) aiming the Samson's 30-caliber door gun on its arm mount.

ABOVE: (row one, left to right) CARB system submachine gun; blasting compound from the mine; Bush Boss Chem/Therm Incinerator flamethrower; (row two, left to right) SecOps knife; CARB system shotgun/20mm munitions launcher; CARB system submachine gun with optical sight; (row three, left to right) CARB system assault rifle; standard-issue SecOps pistol, 30-caliber door gun from Samson Tiltrotor; (row four, left to right) Samson rocket; belt-feed ammunition for AMP Suit; fragmentation grenade; (row five, left to right) submachine gun; CARB system assault rifle; incendiary grenade.

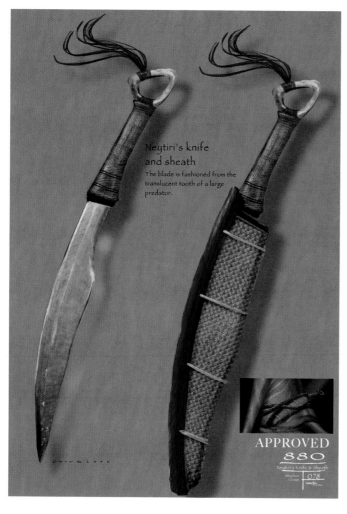

Neytiri's knife
and sheath
The blade is fashioned from the translucent tooth of a large predator.

APPROVED
880
Neytiri's Knife & Sheath
Stephen Crowe | 078 | weta

NA'VI ARROW
(USED BY NEYTIRI
IN SPRITE SCENE)

Plant gum arrowhead bound to
wooden arrow shaft.

Arrow approx. 5' long.

880
Neytiri's (Na'vi)
Arrow
D. Falconer | 663 | weta

JAKE'S NA'VI ARROW

Plant resin (gum) arrowhead with
insect-wing fletching.

Approx. 5' long.

880
Jake's Na'vi Arrow
D. Falconer
N. Keller | 718 | weta

880
Jake's Knife
Tobin | 157 | weta

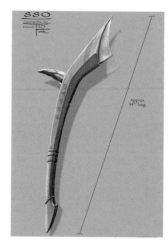

880
Hunting War Bow
Weta | 525 | weta

Approx. 54" long

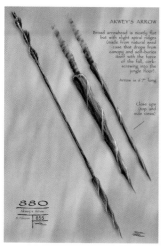

AKWEY'S ARROW

Broad arrowhead is mostly flat
but with eight spiral ridges
(made from natural seed
case that drops from
canopy and self-buries
itself with the force
of the fall, cork-
screwing into the
jungle floor).

Arrow is 6'7" long.

Close ups
(top and
side views)

Close up

880
Akwey's Arrow
D. Falconer | 655 | weta

NA'VI FISHING ARROW

Barbed wooden spines
bound to shaft of arrow.

Fletching is intricately bound
feather-like tufts on an
arched filament.

Thread prevents fish
from escaping with
arrow imbedded.

Arrow approx.
5' long.

Close up

880
Na'vi Fishing
Arrow
D. Falconer | 667 | weta

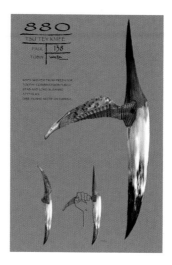

880
TSU'TEY KNIFE
PAUL | 158
TOBIN | weta

KNIFE SHAPED FROM PREDATOR
TOOTH. COMBINATION PUNCH
STAB AND LONG SLASHING
ATTACKS.
ONE-HANDED MOTIF ON HANDLE.

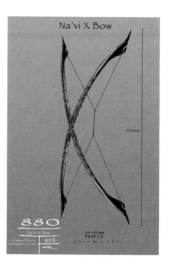

Na'vi X Bow

2500mm

880
Na'vi X Bow
Christian Pearce
& Stephen Crowe | 605 | weta

OPPOSITE: Early study of the Na'vi culture (Messing).

THIS PAGE: As conceived by Weta Workshop's designers, Na'vi weapons combined natural jungle resources with superb craftsmanship; the items are both lethally efficient and beautiful. Workshop artists reasoned that the Na'vi would use a variety of materials from their forest home to create tools and weapons, including crystal arrowheads. Neytiri's knife (top left) is carved from the translucent tooth of a jungle predator (by Stephen Crowe).

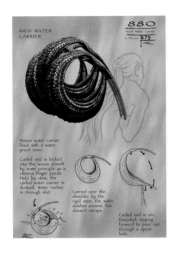

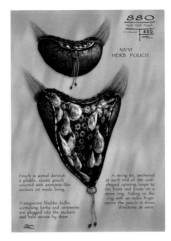

A B O V E : Cameron reviews set props at the offices of Weta Workshop. Weta Digital principle Joe Letteri stands to the left; Carter stands to Cameron's right. To his left is Weta Workshop's co-founder, Richard Taylor, and costume supervisor Matt Appleton (mid-February 2007).

OPPOSITE, BOTTOM: Na'vi textiles designer Claire Prebble.

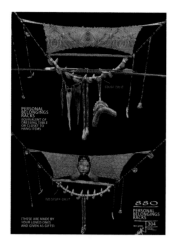

Having theorized that the Na'vi had developed the art of weaving to very high levels, Weta Workshop's artists integrated complex and intricate woven designs into many of the props they created for the film. All props were finished as digital assets; many were also physically built, at Na'vi size.

OPPOSITE, TOP and LEFT: Weta's early studies explore the hunting-and-gathering lifestyle of the Na'vi.

ABOVE: Final war paint designs by Seth Engstrom.

OPPOSITE: Final battle with Quaritch in front of the Shack (frame grabs), along with images from the original performance-capture sessions (INSET).

Weta Workshop also built set pieces for the live-action shoot, such as the Link Units the human drivers use to connect to their avatar bodies. Workshop crews initiated the link-unit build by creating a 3-D digital model of Rick Carter's design. From that 3-D model the artists built a one-sixth-scale prototype. "We worked out design issues on that one-sixth model," said Taylor, "and took that to America to show to Jim. Then, when we got back to New Zealand, we used that to figure out all of the very complex mechanisms necessary to make the whole thing work." The Workshop built five Link Units, each a triumph of mechanical engineering, with hoods that opened and closed just so, and mechanisms enabling them to slide to and fro at different speeds and stop on cue. "What looked like a fairly simple piece of operation actually required a lot of complicated mechanical engineering, and, of course, because it is equipment from the future, we had to hide all of the components within a very tight canopy."

The single-most difficult aspect of building the Link Units, however, was creating their slightly glowing, translucent, gelatinous interiors. Taylor knew that most commercially available gel materials would deteriorate under the hot lights of movie production, and finding a suitable material turned into a very taxing problem. Taylor finally made contact with a company in Los Angeles that had developed a soft, gel-like material most commonly used for padded bras. Taylor arranged for the material to be produced in mass quantities and sent to New Zealand, where his crew fashioned it into the link-unit beds.

Set design for *Avatar*'s live action shoot in New Zealand was overseen by production designer Rick Carter; the sets and special set pieces were built by Weta Workshop and the New Zealand Art Department, run by art director Kim Sinclair. Among the Hell's Gate interiors were Grace's Bio Lab, the Link Room, and its adjacent Ambient Room, in which Jake wakes up in his avatar body. The Ops Center, the nerve center from which Selfridge runs the human operation on Pandora, was another major set. Elsewhere within the base are the enormous Armor Bay, which is Quaritch's turf, and the Commissary, in which Quaritch briefs the fresh arrivals to Pandora—each was designed and built under the direction of Carter and Sinclair. Other sets included the Shack (built inside and out), a jungle set, as well as the Valkyrie shuttle cargo bay, the Dragon cockpit, and the Samson. Other significant full-size set props that required extensive pre-planning, design, and construction included the Amnio Tanks and the Link Units, as seen here.

OPPOSITE: Finished Link Unit in the remote research station known as "the Shack." Weta Workshop built these fully operational Link Units based on designs by Procter, who created a highly plausible look to the futuristic technology.

ABOVE, TOP: Cameron shooting with the Fusion camera.

ABOVE, BOTTOM: Worthington as Jake in his final moment before departing the link room and life as he has known it (early December 2007).

OPPOSITE: Low-angle view onto the finished link room set (Stone Street Studios, Wellington, New Zealand). To conserve resources, only half of the circular link room set was built, but multiple camera angles were easily achieved by rotating the center console platform. Digital set extensions completed the set.

ABOVE: Worthington and Moore survey the Ambient Room set from behind its pressurized windows. Unlike the Bio Lab and link room—both set up for human occupation—the Ambient Room is designed for avatars and contains toxic Pandora atmosphere.

Weta Workshop also built two Amnio Tanks, in which the avatars for Jake and Norm are introduced, floating in a bluish fluid. The Amnio Tanks were built of steel and acrylic, the latter rolled into a tubular shape by an industrial firm in Los Angeles. "We found only one company in the world that could actually roll the size of acrylic tube we needed for that," said Taylor. "We had those tubes rolled and shipped to New Zealand, and then we built the engineering around them. This wasn't just model-making. It took a year to build those two units." The build was simplified only slightly by the fact that Cameron never intended actually to fill the amnio tanks with fluid; rather, everything inside the tank—avatar and amniotic fluid— would be computer generated.

Taylor was gratified by Cameron's response to the Amnio Tanks when the director arrived for the live-action shoot. After walking around them, inspecting them carefully, and challenging Taylor with a few questions, he gave the Amnio Tanks an unequivocal thumbs-up. Another set piece built by Weta Workshop was the exterior of the Samson helicopter. Again, the crew built it first in smaller scale to work out design and mechanical issues. From that five-foot-long model, the Workshop built a full-size fiberglass helicopter shell that measured twenty feet long.

These set pieces, built by Weta Workshop, dressed out the large-scale live-action Hell's Gate environments built by Rick Carter and the New Zealand art department. In the months prior to the live-action shoot, Carter, in Los Angeles, had orchestrated the building of sets in Wellington via video conferencing and FTP sites, sending designs to the New Zealand crew as they were approved. Yuri Bartoli, who had been one of the four concept artists on the production at its earliest stages, modeled these set designs in 3-D in the computer to help Carter determine how much would have to be built practically and what could be left to CG set extensions. Cameron "walked" those sets, virtually, using the capture Volume in Playa Vista as a previsualization tool. He was able to "scout" the sets with the live-action director of photography, Mauro Fiore, and choose all the camera and lighting positions prior to ever laying eyes on the real thing being built in Wellington.

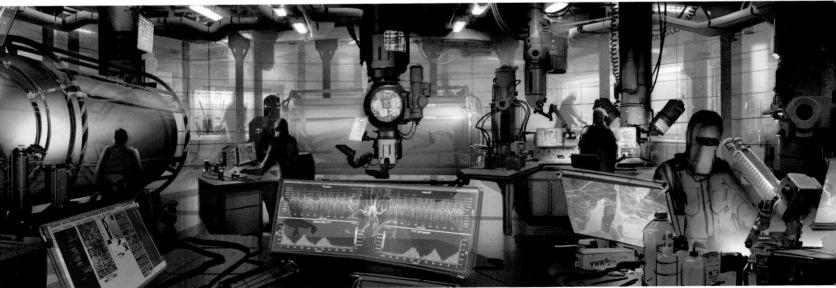

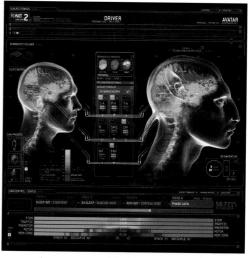

OPPOSITE, TOP: Cameron working out the initial scene where Jake (Worthington) and Norm (Moore) first enter the Bio Lab and are presented with their avatars by Dr. Max Patel (Dileep Rao).

OPPOSITE, BOTTOM: Early development of the Bio Lab by James Clyne.

ABOVE, TOP LEFT: This Lightstorm rendering incorporates design geometry by Procter, Victor Martinez, and Scott Baker.

ABOVE, TOP RIGHT: A key to demonstrating the link between avatar and human driver were the screen graphics on the translucent monitors. This layout by Procter culminates an array of exploratory designs by Clyne, Leri Greer, and Aaron Beck. The motion-graphics firm Prime Focus later contributed animation and three-dimensionality. Los Angeles–based fabricators realized the transparent computer displays using pieces of curved Plexiglas. For background monitors, graphics consisted of transparencies backed by a thin electroluminescent (EL) film; for foreground workstations, graphics were applied in post production as visual effects.

ABOVE, BOTTOM: An early illustration by Clyne suggested a dark and moody ambience for the link room, but already showed the radial array of Link Units surrounding a central core of control stations.

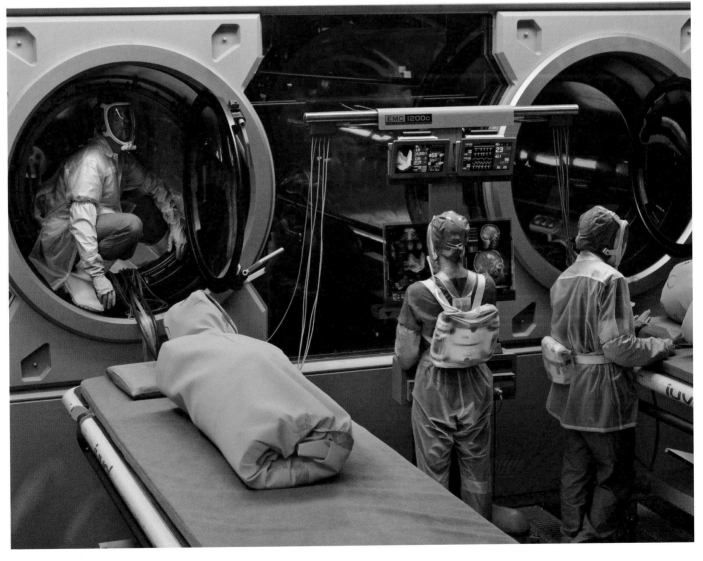

For film production projects as vast as *Avatar*, the design process is often highly collaborative; the Ambient Room is no exception. Although detailed largely by Scott Baker and Ben Procter, the Ambient Room's interior (OPPOSITE, TOP), by Procter, incorporated the previous designs of James Clyne, Victor Martinez, and Kevin Ishioka. Its final construction is shown here (OPPOSITE, BOTTOM); Link Units have been connected and the actors are prepping for the scene in which Jake and Norm wake up in their avatar bodies. Note the detailed MedTech costumes, including slightly futuristic medical masks and backpacks.

ABOVE: The practical Amnio Tanks, in which embryonic avatars develop to maturity, had a docking ring and hatch on one end, which allowed mounting to complementary ports on the Ambient Room window wall. This also allowed the "decanting" of avatars directly into a Pandoran atmosphere (the technological equivalent of birth for an avatar). Frosted Plexiglas and a light source stood in for residual liquid at the bottom of the tank. Shots of fluid-filled tanks required Weta Digital to digitally simulate the embryonic fluid and the submerged avatar's interaction with it.

OVERLEAF: Amid freshly sprayed tank interiors, Cameron pauses to review activity in the Ambient Room (mid-December 2007).

Practical Hell's Gate sets took up forty thousand square feet of floor space at the studio and included an armor bay, laboratory, operations center, and link room. Other sets were the "Shack" at Site 26—the remote science station located among the floating mountains—plus ten thousand square feet of practical rain forest built at a Weta annex in what was once a Mitsubishi car factory. "We built that forest set initially," said Jon Landau, "because we didn't know at the beginning how successful we would be in putting human characters into CG environments. There was a scene in the movie, which didn't make it into the final cut, where Quaritch leads the troops into the jungle for the first time. A lot of that jungle set was going to be used for that sequence, and later in the battle. But as we got into the film we realized that we were much better off putting practical elements in front of a green or blue screen and adding the depth of the scene digitally."

The art department designed Hell's Gate to be a familiar-seeming "near future" rather than wildly futuristic, to ground the viewer in contrast to the phantasmagorical imagery of wild Pandora. They fashioned vending machines,

for example, based on state-of-the-art units seen mostly in Japan. "We would discuss where things like that were going," said supervising art director Kim Sinclair, "and then put a little twist on it, but nothing radical, because Jim didn't want anything that would distract the audience from the story. It was all very much about the people and the characters, rather than the sets."

To save time and money and allow for maximum camera access, Carter and his crews built only half of the circular Link Room, with a green screen enclosing the other half of the semicircle, into which digital set extensions would be added in postproduction. "Jim decided that it was better to build half the set with great quality and design than have the whole set half-built," commented Mauro Fiore. "There was just an unbelievable amount of detail in the sets—railings and supports and the fasteners on the link beds—all these specific little elements. It wasn't simply showing up at a hardware store and picking out the parts. All the details, all the bolts and screws, all the locks on the doors were designed specifically for the film. I've never seen anything as thoroughly designed in any Hollywood film I've worked on."

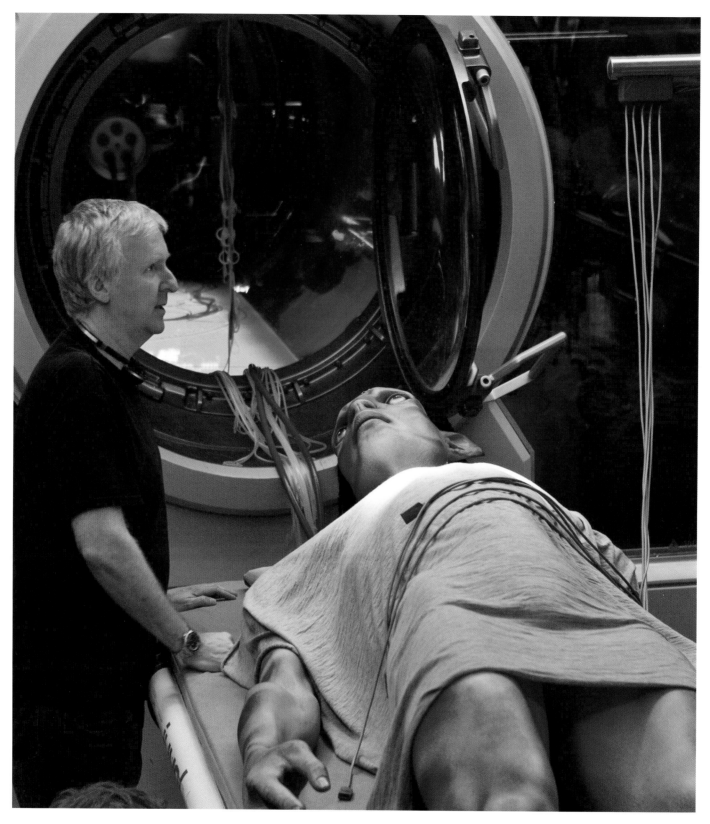

OPPOSITE: Weta Digital's floating avatar melds seamlessly into this final shot, in part because of the breakthrough performance interactivity allowed by Simulcam (see pages 226–229 for more detail).

ABOVE: Cameron in the Ambient Room preparing for a Simulcam session; for this scene, Jake's avatar has recently been fully "decanted" out of its Amnio Tank—still-attached via the open-hatched circular airlock in the background. The Winston Studio avatar-size full-body model is being used to set proportions and placement for the cameras and eyelines. For actual shooting, the Ambient Room MedTechs act against an empty space. Nearby, Worthington and Moore conduct a performance-capture session for this scene, which is then live-composited into the Ambient Room in Cameron's viewfinder, a technique known on the production as "Simulcam."

If Hell's Gate is a body, then the Ops Center is its brain. Located inside the control tower, it's conceived as an informational and tactical nerve center for all mining and military efforts on Pandora.

ABOVE, TOP: Two dimensional painting by Clyne (2006).

ABOVE, BOTTOM: Cameron working with a small HD camera during a day of live-action shooting in the Ops Center (mid-November 2007). The small camera was used during initial rehearsals to help determine the actual shots, similar to how directors used to use a viewfinder.

OPPOSITE, TOP: Jake and Quaritch study the structural vulnerabilities of the Na'vi Hometree on the Ops Center's HoloTable. The design of the table's holographics was developed by Aaron Beck and Leri Greer of Weta Workshop. Simulcam was used for HoloTable shots so Cameron and his actors could see a live rendition of the table's graphic content composited over the camera feed. Table design by Procter; table projection bed by Tex Kadonaga.

OPPOSITE, BOTTOM: Worthington and Lang perform a scene in which Jake brings back intel about the Na'vi; green-screen background was filled by both physical translight paintings and with CG environments from visual effects houses during post production (late November 2007).

The construction crews also built practical sections of aircraft such as the Samson and the Dragon. At the beginning, the art department in New Zealand literally had no idea how to go about building the ships, as typical wood-framing techniques wouldn't suffice for such complex geometries. After doing extensive research into how real aircraft are built, the art department decided that their best bet would be to build their aircraft in the same way, in riveted aluminum. "We cheated a bit," Kim Sinclair admitted. "There's a bit of steel in it, and there's a lot more welding than an aircraft engineer would approve of, but that's how we built the Samson." Everything on the Samson, save a few pieces scavenged from a Black Hawk helicopter, was built from scratch. "The Samson was very realistic. It felt and smelled like a real aircraft, and all the buttons were wired up. We worked out all the protocols for starting the Samson and shutting it down."

To simulate flight for interior Samson shots of pilots at the controls, the filmmakers mounted the craft to a hydraulic motion base. For exterior shots, such as when Trudy's Samson delivers Grace, Jake, and Norm to the remote Site 26, they hung it from a crane and landed it on a set of the landing field built on the back lot of the studio. "We had air movers blowing the grass as it really would if a helicopter landed," Jon Landau recalled. A green screen erected behind the practical landing area allowed the background of the Hallelujah Mountains to be digitally composited later.

The art department also built the forward section of the Dragon gunship, as well as the cargo bay and loading ramp of the Valkyrie space shuttle, the latter for shots of Jake, Norm, and the others being transported to Pandora. The shuttle interior was made mostly of aluminum and was painstakingly detailed following reference images of real C-17 military transports.

"There was real artistry available in New Zealand for this movie," said Jon Landau. "What Richard Taylor and Weta Workshop and Kim Sinclair and the art department were able to bring to the table was remarkable. Jim has said that he's never worked on sets better than those. The people working there brought not just artistry, but a real passion for this movie. If you asked them to create something, they never just created it, they came up with the 'why' it was created."

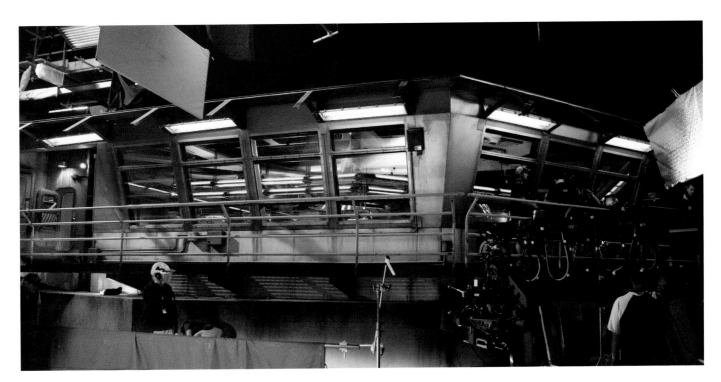

ABOVE: The Ops Center exterior set catwalk, based on designs by Martinez, incorporating designs from Martinez, Clyne, and Sam Page.

OPPOSITE, TOP: Selfridge in his office—an extension of the Ops Center set (frame grab).

OPPOSITE, BOTTOM: Cameron directing the scene in which this remote tractor operator (actor Kevin Dorman) is about to plough a mining vehicle through the willow glade.

OPPOSITE, TOP: Armor bay concept painting by Clyne.

OPPOSITE, BOTTOM: A wide-angle view of the finished armor bay set; note the Samson mock-up in the distant background (early November 2007).

ABOVE, TOP: Pilot Trudy Chacon (Michelle Rodriguez) leads Jake through the Armor Bay. Winston Studio's full-sized AMP Suit stands on the left, surrounded by maintenance crew. Wellington, New Zealand (early November 2007).

ABOVE, BOTTOM: Frame grab of same scene.

Landau (OPPOSITE) and Cameron (ABOVE, BOTTOM LEFT) on set for the exterior at Stone Street Studios; Cameron is speaking with director of photography Mauro Fiore (late January 2008). In the entire production of *Avatar*, there was only one day and one night of exterior photography, and the night was "night-for-day" so that the look of daylight under dense jungle canopy could be simulated.

ABOVE, TOP: Cameron shooting with the Fusion 3-D camera on set inside Stone Street Studios in New Zealand with actresses Rodriguez (pilot Trudy Chacon) and Weaver (Dr. Grace Augustine), mid-December 2007. A few weeks later (ABOVE, BOTTOM RIGHT), Cameron on the same set; first assistant director and co-producer Josh McLagen stands to his left.

ABOVE, TOP: Another live-action set built at Stone Street was the cargo bay of the Valkyrie shuttle. Here, the view is looking aft toward the open ramp during the final battle, as the aircrew moves the "daisycutter" pallets into position to drop on the Tree of Souls.

ABOVE, BOTTOM: Nighttime view of the exterior green-screen set at Stone Street Studios in New Zealand.

OPPOSITE: Cameron directing the stuntmen prior to the "helo insertion" of troops into the rainforest, at the start of the final battle.

OVERLEAF: Wide-angle view of the exterior green-screen set at Stone Street Studios (late January 2008). The only exterior set created for the film, it is shown here dressed as the mountain meadow at Site 26, in which the Samson lands near the Shack. Later, the set was redressed as a jungle, for the landing scene in which ground troops are deployed prior to the final battle. High-powered wind machines would blow the grass, to simulate the rotor-wash of the Samson as it landed. The Samson mockup was built by Steve Ingram like a real helicopter airframe, so that it would be safe for actors when it was lifted high in the air and swung in, by the crane, for a landing. A 1,500-pound drop-weight was used to change the vehicle's pitch angle between approach and takeoff.

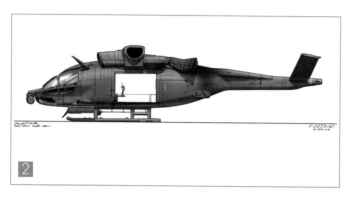

SA-2 SAMSON TILTROTOR

The SA-2 Samson Tiltrotor was an important "character" in its own right. While the Scorpion is a smaller, more nimble, one-man combat aircraft, the Samson is a workhorse, providing transport to remote locales for cargo, SecOps troops, scientists, and avatars. This no-nonsense, heavy-lift, twin-turbine, VTOL rotorcraft has a pressurized cockpit and an open-back bay. Armed with doorguns and missile pods, it is used by pilot Trudy Chacon to airlift the mobile link station deep into the forest and to attack Quaritch's Dragon in the final battle—all while flying "VFR" (Visual Flight Rules) in the Flux Vortex, which scrambles her instruments.

Its design was clearly influenced by the iconic Huey helicopters of the Vietnam War, as well as the Blackhawks currently in use in Iraq and Afghanistan; it needed to feel familiar and comfortable, but also seem like aircraft technology of the future. The early design passes were exported to the VAD in a back-and-forth, 2-D-to-3-D design process. This dynamic dialogue allowed the art department to see very rough "video-game-level" work-in-progress Samsons flying in virtual environments—and then go back and make design revisions as needed.

TyRuben Ellingson's final design was the culmination of these efforts, and his "turnover package" (FIGURE 1) was the foundation for the physical and CG builds that followed. His drawings and specifications—as well as CAD files created by the art department—went to the New Zealand Art Department, where the Samson was built and configured for its three live-action modes: sitting on the tarmac, hanging from a crane, or mounted on a motion base.

Weta Digital began the process of creating accurate, high-resolution digital models by referencing these detailed drawings from the art department as well as generating survey data, photographs, and hand measurements of the full-size mockup. The full-scale Samson mockup was built by physical effects supervisor Steve Ingram, overseen by lead supervising art director Kim Sinclair and construction supervisor Neil Kirkland. It incorporated flight control sticks and pedals from actual helicopters, rigged to feel and move like the real thing. Later, Weta Digital constructed a CG version that precisely matched the physical Samson set for all the exterior angles in which the ship was seen at medium distance and beyond. Stephen Rosenbaum consulted with Cameron in the course of digital development; in latter stages, Joe Letteri would present final Samson designs within film shots—based on feedback from Cameron, any necessary final refinements were then applied.

The images here demonstrate some of the key stages in the evolution of the final designs. FIGURE 2 is a paintover by illustrator Paul Ozzimo of Ellingson's sketch-up model—showing skin detail. FIGURE 3 is a digital rendering showing (in green) the portions of the Samson that would be extended as CG elements—specifically the tail and rotor assemblies. FIGURE 4 is a high-resolution model by Weta Digital that exactly matches the physical Samson set, followed by FIGURE 5, a depiction of this same high-resolution model with painted texture maps applied.

OPPOSITE: Cameron and McLaglen discuss the troop landing scene, as the Samson mockup hangs on the crane (Wellington, late January 2008).

OVERLEAF: Development art of Na'vi on the Pandoran plains at night.

ABOVE: The Shack set at the Warehouse in New Zealand.

OPPOSITE, TOP: Preparing with actors Weaver and Worthington.

OPPOSITE, BOTTOM: Cameron shooting with the Fusion "handheld rig" in the Shack.

Costume designers Mayes C. Rubeo and Deborah Lynn Scott, too, considered the "why" as they created thousands of costume pieces for the Hell's Gate science, mining, and military crews. One of the goals of the designers was to create costumes that would subtly suggest the film's 2154 time setting but would still resonate with audiences. "When someone walked out of an elevator," said New Zealand costumer John Harding, "we needed to know that they were a truck driver or a biologist or a scientist. There was no point in putting them in silver lamé spacesuits or catsuits or strange asymmetrical jackets. We just made very real, normal stuff. I don't believe that denim will ever go out of fashion. I don't believe the T-shirt will ever go out of fashion."

Costume designs were influenced by the clothing's function: What did the clothes worn by various Hell's Gate teams have to *do*? And so, in their avatar forms, Jake, Grace, and Norm, for example, wear photographer's vests and pocketed cargo pants to hold their science gear. The climate also influenced costume designs. "We cut the sleeves off," said Harding, "and ripped off all the buttons, as if [the characters] were trying to let some air in." The heat was also suggested, by bleaching the clothing of characters that spend a lot of time outdoors. "We created really neat faded summer clothing, as if [to suggest that] these people have been there a long time and all the color has drained out of their clothes."

RDA security forces, called SecOps Troopers, wore uniforms inspired by classic military looks, such as those worn by soldiers in the Vietnam era, but with a bit of irreverence mixed in to support the idea of these soldiers as mercenaries who operate outside the strict rules of a traditional military. The costumers also signified the various ranks of the military corps, subtly altering the insignia of American military ranks. "[There are both] noncommissioned officers and commissioned officers," said Harding, "and Jim wanted, at a glance, to know which was which. He wanted you to know who were the guys with guns." Camouflage patterns on uniforms were designed with very straight lines to contrast with the curved lines of the Na'vi costuming. This "digital camouflage" was a futuristic detail that the designers created, only to see it adopted later, coincidentally, by U.S. military fashion. The designers created interesting texture in the uniforms by giving them a crumpled look. "We just about banned ironing in the future! No one irons anything, because in 3-D, especially, all that texture looked fantastic."

The costumers also built Na'vi garments as reference pieces for the CG artists at Weta Digital, adding to the sample pieces created by Weta Workshop. "I would sketch out a design," explained Deborah Lynn Scott, "and then have a couple of people make a three-dimensional item. I worked with Photoshop artists at the same time. So Jim got to see it in that space, and also see part or all of a piece in 3-D."

"We could have just done a drawing and given it to digital, and said, 'This is it. Make this,'" said John Harding, "but a drawing wouldn't have told the CG artists how that garment would hang, what its weight was, how it would move in wind. All of that is information you can't expect a technician in a darkened room in front of a screen to know from a drawing." The designers used unusual laser-cutting techniques, atypical cutting patterns, and exotic gauzy materials, to construct hundreds of sample garments that would look as if they hadn't been made on Earth by human hands. "We used a lot of fine rayon and silk combinations in beautiful, twisted weaves to get something that almost floats," said Harding.

Just as Weta Workshop derived inspiration for Na'vi weapons from the plant and animal life available on Pandora, the costumers based their Na'vi garments and adornments on that natural world. "The Na'vi get their clothing from the nature around them," commented Mayes C. Rubeo. "They kill for protein, but they don't dispose of the [animal remains]. They use the leather, the bones. They also use things from plants and trees." Fur pelts were not used on any of the costumes, since Cameron had established that the creatures of Pandora are furless. Feathers were used for decorative purposes, though—painted rooster feathers and those from exotic tropical birds, painted and dyed to create colors that wouldn't be seen on Earth. The crew also hand-painted bits of wood, glass, and seeds for the Na'vi beading, devising unusual, asymmetrical looks that didn't match that of any known Earth culture.

After designing and building sample costuming pieces at human scale, the costumers put them on tall, thin models so that Cameron could see them on moving subjects. The costume crew also put costume pieces on the human-size Na'vi mannequins that Stan Winston Studio had provided to production. Once Cameron approved a costume, it would be thoroughly photographed—moving and in various poses, sometimes blown by wind machines—and those reference images would go to Weta Digital, which used them to model the digital clothing.

LEFT: The live-action jungle set was outfitted with various alien plants, including several full-size versions of this pod-covered dapophet—a common Pandoran succulent. Sinclair and the New Zealand Art Department oversaw the creation of all live-action sets, which included several full-size hero versions of this pod-covered tree fern, as well as all other plants, greens, and trees that surrounded the Shack.

BELOW, TOP: Dr. Grace Augustine (Weaver) gathering samples in the open Pandoran air.

BELOW, BOTTOM: Inside the fully built Shack interior, shooting carried on for several weeks. Cameron is operating the Fusion 3-D camera while Rodriguez, Worthington, Moore, and Weaver perform a scene.

In mid-September on the stage at Playa Vista, property master Andy Siegel shows Stephen Rosenbaum how Worthington will sit in the wheelchair when his rubber prosthetic legs are used during live-action filming (**ABOVE**). On set in the Shack, in early November 2007, Worthington practices entering and exiting the Link Unit as a paraplegic (**OPPOSITE, TOP LEFT**); his prosthetic legs, created by Winston Studio, were molded from the legs of a paralyzed man whose height matched Worthington's. This ensured medical accuracy regarding muscle atrophy due to long-term paralysis (**OPPOSITE, TOP RIGHT**). Worthington, Weaver, and Moore in the Shack (**OPPOSITE, BOTTOM**).

RIGHT: In this set photo, Worthington's legs can be seen below the seat of the chair, clad in green Lycra. They will be removed digitally later, leaving only the rubber prosthetic legs visible. Though there are only two shots of the prosthetic limbs in the final cut, Sam's performance even fooled real paraplegics into thinking he was paralyzed. After the premiere of the film, a wheelchair-bound man in the audience, obviously unfamiliar with Worthington's prior work, asked the director who the new "chair actor" was.

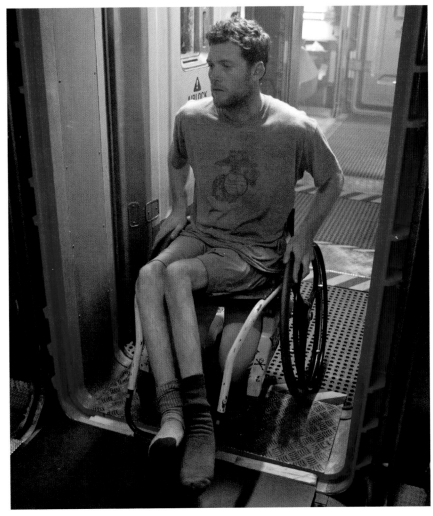

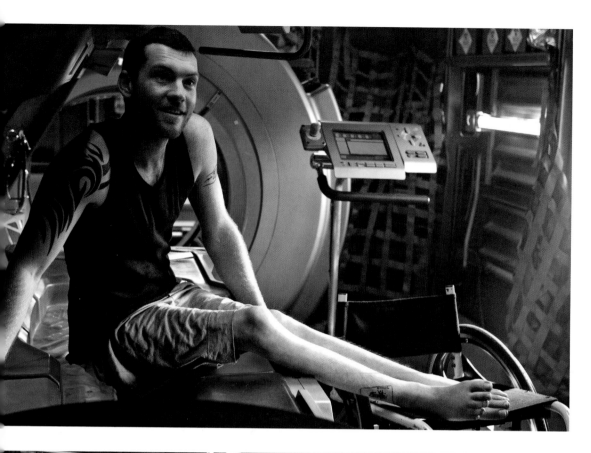

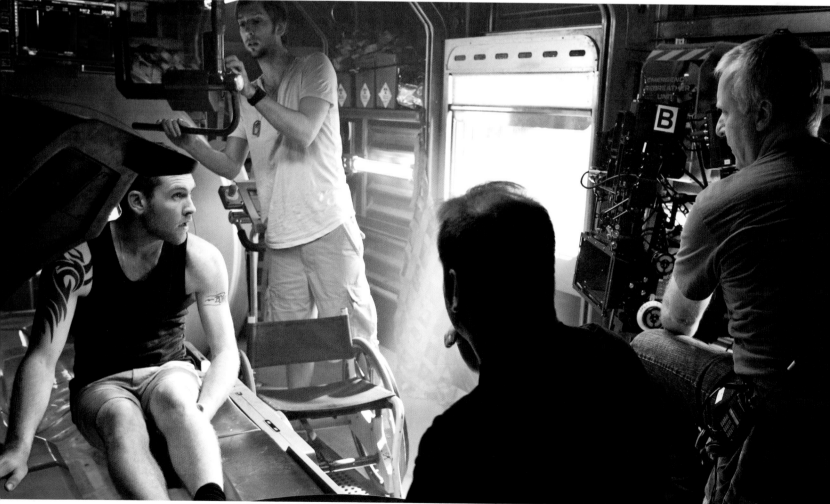

Costumes, props, and sets were all in various stages of completion by the time the shoot with Cameron and Mauro Fiore commenced in October 2007. One of the first live-action scenes to be shot was Jake's meeting with Quaritch in the armor bay. The scene featured two Stan Winston Studio makeup effects: the three long claw scars on the side of Quaritch's head and face, and Jake's atrophied legs. "Jim wanted unique scars on Quaritch," said John Rosengrant. "We worked out the look in Photoshop and did a test on Stephen Lang in Los Angeles prior to the shoot in New Zealand. He was up for whatever it took, so we shaved into his real hair to put those prosthetic scars on his scalp. It was supposed to look like something with huge claws nearly took off the side of his head."

To create Jake's withered legs, Winston artists cast the legs of a paraplegic combat veteran and made leg prosthetics from those casts. The legs would be most prominently on display in a scene in which Jake lifts himself up into

A

lens variation 01

PROJECT 880
TSU-TEY VISOR
12.28.2006 · ShOJI

While riding motorcycles one morning with friend Arnold Schwarzenegger, Cameron began thinking about the force of wind in the eyes of the Na'vi flyers. He experimented with the visor on his helmet to find a position in which he could see under it at low wind speeds, with eyes exposed to the wind, or look through it at higher speeds, cocking his head downward. This formed the basis of the Na'vi flight visor. At airspeeds above 100 knots, the characters look through their visors, made of transparent insect wings. At lower speeds, with heads raised, they look under the edge of the visor. Under the direction of Stromberg and Engstrom, former intern Craig Shoji took a first crack at designing Cameron's visor; he also experimented with shards of bone and talons for ornamentation. Academy Award®–winning costume designer Deborah Scott revised the concept; the final version retained this central bone piece, which gives Jake a bird-of-prey appearance.

ABOVE: Flight visor initial concept design by Shoji. ABOVE, INSET: Final design by Scott, as seen on a bust of Jake; costumer Claire Prebble crafted the texture sample, and costumer Rafael Bugos—with Scott's direction—combined the elements in a Photoshop file, which, along with physical samples, were shipped off to Weta Digital. OPPOSITE: Jake looking through his visor during an attack dive in the final battle.

the Link Unit, wearing shorts, and later when he wheels himself through the corridors of the Shack. "When he was getting into the link and you saw his legs," explained Jon Landau, "his body was positioned in a hole in the link itself, and the prosthetics were attached in front of him. That was a clean, nondigital shot. When he was in the wheelchair, he was wearing green tights on his real legs, which were tucked under the wheelchair, and the prosthetics, again, [were] attached in front of him. And then we had to do digital cleanup of the exposed green areas." Worthington also wore caps on his knees in shots in which his legs were covered, which made his legs look thinner and smaller in comparison to the oversize kneecaps.

Cameron and Fiore shot all of the live action with a new-and-improved version of the Fusion 3D camera rig that Cameron had developed over a seven-year period with engineering partner Vince Pace. Even while employing the 3-D camera system for his underwater documentaries and other projects, Cameron knew he would one day want to make a state-of-the-art stereoscopic feature film—something that was still a rarity in mainstream Hollywood films at the time he went into development on *Avatar*. "There hadn't been a main kind of tent-pole movie made in live-action 3-D yet," said Cameron. "*Avatar* was going to be the test case."

By the time Cameron was ready to shoot *Avatar*'s live action, the Fusion camera rig had evolved into a very

OPPOSITE: Quaritch (Stephen Lang) briefs the new arrivals on the dangers of Pandora (December 2007).

ABOVE: Cameron shooting the scene with the Fusion 3-D camera on a dolly.

flexible, production-friendly tool. "Jim wanted the technology to be transparent during the shoot," said Vince Pace. "Of course, making the technology transparent would be much easier with a director who mainly works off a crane or a dolly. Jim loves camera movement. He likes to have it on his shoulder right next to an actor as he's talking to him just as much as he likes to fly it in on a Technocrane, and we had to adapt the technology so that he could change from one to the other as quickly as possible. The size of the camera system and the ability to mount it on Technocranes or a Steadicam or [to] operate it handheld were all important for making it workable for production."

A few weeks prior to shooting in New Zealand, Cameron sent Pace a three-page e-mail delineating everything he wanted the 3-D camera rig to do on set, including specifications for the focal length ranges of the zoom lenses, camera frame rates, playback viewing, and even the balancing of the Steadicam system. This spurred Pace and his engineering team to work around the clock to meet all the new requirements within the short time frame. The updated camera rig, like its predecessors, consisted of two synchronized HD cameras and lenses—one shooting the right-eye perspective and the other shooting the left. One camera was rigged to slide on a track to change the distance between the two cameras, which represented the interocular, or distance between the left and right eye. Adjusting that distance would create more or less depth in the final image, and thus a more dramatic or less dramatic stereoscopic effect.

Cameron and Pace had discovered, early in the development process, that it was critical to change the interocular, or "IO," dynamically during the shot, as the distance between the camera and its subject changed. In addition, the camera's optical axes could be changed relative to each other to "toe in" as human eyes do as a subject gets closer. This "convergence" was controlled by servomotors and had to vary dynamically during a moving shot. All of this motion, driven by strong but silent servomotors, was happening while the shot was in progress, often while the camera was perched on Cameron's shoulder. The Fusion camera "breathed" like a living thing, and was as futuristic as anything that was taking place in front of its lenses.

Camera weights and sizes varied, with the most commonly used rig weighing between twenty-five and thirty-three pounds. "The camera is not that much bigger than a standard film camera," Pace explained. The camera rig was electronically configured to operate in upright mode, on a dolly or crane, or to switch rapidly to upside down "inverted mode," for handheld and Steadicam applications. A servo-actuated counterweight was developed so that the cameras would not unbalance the Steadicam rig as it moved to adjust interocular distance. As one camera slid to the right or left dynamically during the shot, the counterweights would automatically slide in the opposite direction to keep the delicately balanced Steadicam rig stable in the operator's hand.

Avatar was Mauro Fiore's first experience as cinematographer on a 3-D film, and so, prior to principal photography, he shot extensive 3-D tests with stand-ins and, later, the actors themselves on small test sets. "I just approached it normally, like I would any film test," said Fiore, "with dramatic lighting on the face. The 3-D aspect was really amazing, because it wasn't simply a flat image that was in front of me. The different accents of light you usually put in just to create depth were already there."

For viewing the 3-D effect during shooting, the crew went to "The Pod," a real-time viewing environment consisting of a small trailer set up as a digital 3-D screening room that was always nearby on stage. In the Pod, a scene could be viewed while it was being shot, or played back immediately after a take. "The image coming from the camera was not a proxy-image from a video-tap," explained Cameron. "The movie was being shot digitally, and the feed from the camera was the final image quality of the movie." Since the Pod used a full-resolution digital cinema projector, the image on screen was identical in quality to what would be seen later in theaters. "The concept of 'dailies' ceased to exist. There was no more waiting a day or so for film to come back from processing at a lab somewhere. 3-D viewing of the final quality image was instantaneous."

"Once we were done shooting a scene," recalled Joel David Moore, "you could just walk fifteen feet away, get yourself into a Pod, put on some glasses, and watch your scene in 3-D."

OPPOSITE, TOP: Cameron and director of photography Mauro Fiore in the 3-D "Pod," built for the production specifically for the immediate viewing of 3-D shots as they are being set up and lit. The Pod was a miniature 3-D theater, with projector and screen, built inside a twenty-foot trailer, which could be positioned very close to the camera setup. Since the Pod had a 2K digital cinema projector, the quality of the image seen at the moment of shooting was exactly as audiences would see it later, except for the missing visual effects. (late December 2007).

OPPOSITE, BOTTOM: Cameron reviewing materials with costume designer Scott.

RIGHT: Derry on the Ops Center set with McLaglen and Landau observing (early November 2007).

BELOW: Monitor view of production-in-process in the Ops Center. Note the difference in backgrounds between the "Mix" in the top screen (Simulcam view) versus the "Clean" view on the bottom, which has only green screen in the background. Image taken by Rosenbaum, late December 2007.

OPPOSITE: Frame grab of same scene.

Geoff Burdick, who had worked on a number of Lightstorm projects, was responsible for checking the quality of the stereo imagery in the Pod for every shot. His comments, delivered via walkie-talkie to Cameron and Fiore on set, allowed fine adjustments of the 3-D to take place without everyone stopping work to run to the Pod. Of course, the real fun of shooting a movie in 3-D was going to the Pod to view a take after hours of work setting up the shot. The Pod was used to solve problems and fine-tune the 3-D.

The stereoscopic effect in shots that were fully CG shots would be achieved in the computer, and both the live-action and CG imagery were the highest-quality 3-D ever created for a film. Still, Cameron was restrained in his use of the stereoscopic effect, rejecting cheap, in-your-face gags in favor of more subtle 3-D enhancements such as flying insects, bioluminescent wood sprites, and glowing fire embers that gently swirled out into the viewerspace. "This wasn't 3-D so we could poke spears in your eye," noted Robert Stromberg. "That wasn't the point. The point was that this was a beautiful, epic jungle, and you wanted to see depth in that jungle. It was a device to give the audience the sense that they were there. The goal was that half an hour into the movie, the audience wouldn't even realize it was 3-D. It was just a window into the world of Pandora."

So far, the technical teams had created two new and completely separate camera systems in order to make *Avatar*. One was the virtual camera, which wasn't a camera at all, in the sense of optics and lenses. The other, the Fusion

camera, was a true camera for real-world photography, but was unlike anything ever built before. For their next trick, the engineers combined the two cameras to create the "Simulcam" system.

"Simulcam" was an interface between the Fusion 3-D rig and the performance-capture system. One of the most groundbreaking aspects of *Avatar*'s production, Simulcam enabled Cameron to see, in his camera monitor, digital characters interacting with live actors on live-action sets.

Typically, one of the biggest challenges of shooting a live-action scene that will feature a CG character is compensating for the fact that the character isn't there at the moment of shooting. Directors and camera operators try to envision where the computer-animated character will be and frame shots accordingly. They count out timings to determine how long it will take a CG character to get from this side of the room to that side of the room so that the camera can track with the character. They set up C-stands or cardboard cutouts at the right height to help actors maintain correct eyelines. Despite all of these efforts, however, shooting a scene with a character that isn't there—and won't be there for months—is an exercise in guessing. Inevitably, the camera work, the actor performances, the interactions, and the sheer dynamics of the scene are compromised by the fact that a central character is missing.

With the advent of real-time performance capture, Cameron saw a way to solve this problem. As far back as 2005, Cameron had queried Glenn Derry about the feasibility of motion-capturing the live-action 3-D cameras on the live-action set, and then feeding an actor's performance, captured nearby in a motion-capture Volume, into that camera's monitor. "If we can capture the motion of this virtual camera," Cameron wondered, "which isn't a camera at all, just an object with markers on it that the computer says is a camera, then why can't we capture a real camera? Why not put markers on the live-action camera, and have the system render on the fly to show us what's not there?" Cameron wanted to stream in not just the CG characters, but the digital set extensions to fill green-screen areas in the live-action set. The result would be that he could shoot his scene with *all* of his characters—live and digital—visible in the viewfinder, all interacting within a complete, rather than partial, set. He would be able to see a real-time composite of the scene, and the real-time movement of his camera in that scene, in his monitor as he was shooting it.

It was a revolutionary idea. And it had never been done before. Glenn Derry thought about it, and talked with his tech team. After an hour he came back, and said, "We can't think of a reason why that won't work." Rob Legato and Derry conducted a test a few days later, putting tracking markers on a small video camera and shooting one of the grips talking to an avatar—portrayed by a stunt double on the other side of the stage, whose performance drove the avatar in real time. "It was a very early prototype of the Simulcam system," said Cameron, "but we got very excited about it."

As exciting as the test was, it took the better part of two years for the Simulcam system to be fully operational—just in time for live-action shooting in Wellington. One of the biggest problems was overcoming the lighting on a live-action set. "Motion-capture Volumes are clinical, sterile places where you've got controlled lighting, and everything is built around the parameters of the performance-capture system," said Derry. "That is the optimal setup for motion capture, but that wasn't the lighting we were going to have on a live-action set. There would be all kinds of very bright lights and color filters on the set, and they would interfere with the infrared light that beams down from the motion-capture camera and reflects off of the markers on the performers' bodies—which is how the camera tracks the movement of the performer." Derry solved the problem by mounting small clusters of high-intensity infrared LEDs to the Fusion camera, replacing the traditional reflective markers with "active markers" that emitted light pulses that were precisely synchronized to the motion-capture camera grid. Those LEDs fired in phase with the motion-capture cameras to essentially cancel out the bright set lighting.

To facilitate Simulcam shots, the crew in Wellington built a mobile performance-capture system that could be moved quickly from one live-action set to another. "We built that performance-capture system into every single set that we worked on," said Derry. "So every time Jim held up his camera, he could look through the eyepiece, and if there was green on set, he wouldn't see green—he'd see the digital set extension. And if there was a Na'vi in the shot, he'd see his Na'vi there in his camera."

OPPOSITE: Cameron operating the Fusion 3-D camera while it is on the Technocrane, late January 2008.

An early use of Simulcam was for the scene in which Neytiri rescues Jake from suffocation in the Shack, at the end of the final battle. The Shack was the first set to be shot, and so, within the first few days, the crew members found themselves shooting one of the most technically complex, and dramatically important, moments in the film. "For Neytiri's rescue," Glenn Derry explained, "we shot Zoë Saldana on a performance-capture setup that was adjacent to the set. And then we tracked the camera in the Shack. As Jim hand-held the camera and moved it around the set, he could see where Neytiri was in the scene the whole time." For other shots, the combined image was displayed on the Steadicam operator's monitor, allowing him to follow the action of Neytiri jumping into the room, from seeing her outside through the window of the Shack, all the way to picking up Jake's lifeless body and reviving him. It was revolutionary—and it convinced Cameron and the visual effects team that this was going to redefine how composite scenes were done from that point onward.

Another scene that benefited from Simulcam was the one in which Jake first awakens in his avatar body in the so-called Ambient Room of the Bio Lab. Anxious to try out his new legs, Jake pulls off EKG leads, stands up, and lurches about the room, as lab technicians and medical staff attempt to restrain him. With Simulcam, Cameron was able to shoot the highly interactive scene with a dynamic, hand-held camera look, always keeping the CG avatar in frame.

On the morning of the live-action shoot of the scene, Cameron shot Sam Worthington—in head rig and motion-capture suit—performing Jake's avatar on a set that was scaled down so that the actor would appear avatar-size in relation. "It was a motion-capture version set, with apple boxes and so forth," recalled Derry, "[which was shot] in an adjacent room [to the live action]. So Jim directed the scene with Sam first." Later that day, when Cameron

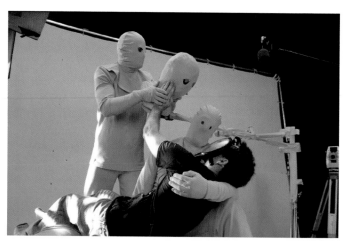

OPPOSITE: Concept painting by Kasra Farahani of Quaritch, in his AMP Suit, attacking the Shack (painted late July 2006).

"This was one of the most difficult shots of the film," says Stephen Rosenbaum. First, a girl who was proportionally the correct scale for a Na'vi to hold a human (0.6 times Worthington's height and weight) was cast. During performance capture (BELOW, TOP LEFT), the girl gave Saldana a body to hold, eyes to look at, and a hand to touch. This performance capture was then played back using Simulcam on the Shack set (LEFT). Cameron saw a low-resolution composite of Neytiri and a proxy Jake (the girl) set against the Shack background in his camera eyepiece and composed the background plate of the Shack as if the characters were really there. Worthington's side of the scene was shot as a green-screen element with the aid of a motion-control system to match the exact camera angle (BELOW, TOP RIGHT).

BOTTOM: Neytiri cradles Jake during their first true meeting, in a shot that was referred to as "the Pieta" (frame grab).

These images, from the scene in which Jake wakes up for the first time in his avatar body, demonstrate the Simulcam system. Simulcam enabled Cameron to shoot the scene as if Jake's avatar was physically on set.

RIGHT: Worthington performing in a Volume adjacent to the live-action set. Julene Renee squats down to simulate the height of her MedTech character, which is indicated by a wire outline, so that Worthington has a correct eyeline. His captured performance is then composited into the camera operator's viewfinder on the Ambient Room live-action set later that day.

BELOW: Cameron uses a pole to create an eyeline for the MedTechs as Jake sits up. He is guided for timing and position by a "real-time composite" image on the monitor, consisting of Worthington's performance capture, rendered by Motion Builder, combined with the live camera image of the room. Cameron would later use a handheld camera to finish the scene, with virtual Jake appearing in his eyepiece.

OPPOSITE, TOP: Cameron and crew gather around the Winston Studio full-size avatar model to assess the space Jake's avatar would require during shooting.

OPPOSITE, BOTTOM: The final frame grab employing this innovative technology.

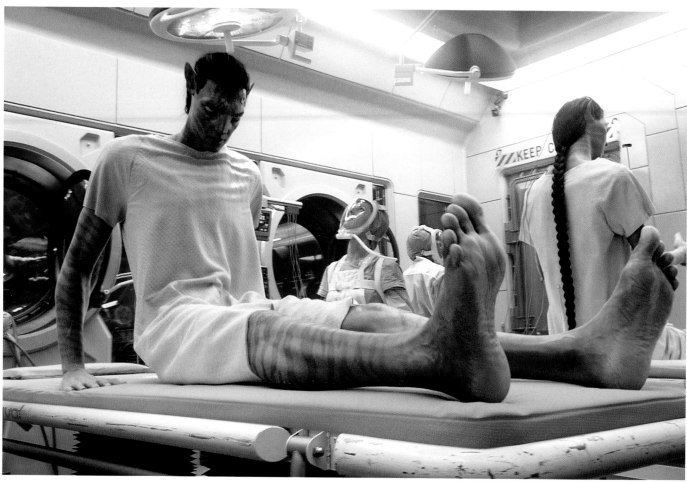

shot the live-action scene, the computer-generated avatar, driven by Worthington's performance from that morning, was there in the room—at least in the eye of the camera. "Jim saw Jake's avatar through his handheld camera eyepiece, through the whole sequence. We played back Sam's performance, and [Jim] could line up to Jake in every shot as he shot on the set. He knew exactly where Jake would be in the shot, so he could frame him and follow him as he wanted."

Of course, though Cameron could see Jake, the actors playing the technicians couldn't; and so a fishing pole was used to create an eyeline as Jake moved around the room, with Cameron calling out cues based on seeing Jake's movements in the eyepiece. It took a few rehearsals, but the final effect was a natural and organic integration of a CG character into a live-action scene.

Simulcam suffered from all the bugs present in any innovative technology, but it proved to be such a liberating tool, and such a cool toy, that Cameron used it whenever it was justified in a scene. Even if a live-action scene had no CG characters but required digital extensions, Cameron would most often call for Simulcam so he could see the complete environment through his camera. Frequent use eventually led to some improvements in the system. "Simulcam was always glitchy; it was always a pain in the ass—and it was always so wonderful when it worked," said Cameron. "We just had to keep beating on it with a stick through the whole process of live action, and eventually we got it dialed in."

While performance capture and the film's stereoscopic format would garner far more attention from the press in the months leading up to and after *Avatar*'s release, as far as Cameron was concerned, Simulcam was the production's most significant technical innovation, if for no other reason than it had the greatest potential for widespread application in the film industry. Very few films would have a need for performance capture—how many movies have ten-foot-tall blue-skinned aliens as their stars?—but

ABOVE: A Simulcam monitor view of Rosenbaum walking through the "clearcutting set" where the bulldozers have been burned by the Na'vi in an ambush, in retaliation for destroying the Tree of Voices glade. The ground is a pincushion of arrows from the aerial attack. Rosenbaum holds up "the balls"—which were recorded at the end of every setup as a way to evaluate the lighting within a live-action shot so that it might be accurately re-created in CG. The gray sphere on the left shows light direction, color temperature, and intensity. The mirrored sphere to the right reflects the light positions. In order to problem-solve how to shoot each scene, Rosenbaum would regularly collaborate with multiple departments: camera, lighting, art, grip, wardrobe, construction, Simulcam, special effects, props, and A.D. Ultimately, the goal—and Weta Digital's responsibility—was to successfully combine this live-action photography with visual effects.

Simulcam would enable filmmakers to integrate CG environments and characters with live-action photography in virtually any visual-effects film.

"Movies such as *Sin City* and *300* have shown that physical sets are becoming a thing of the past," said Cameron, "and most movies these days, even those that are not thought of as major 'effects films,' are using green-screen to create environments and add production value. As these techniques become the standard of the industry, Simulcam and its successors will become commonplace productions tools."

As Cameron and his production crews were shooting and breaking new ground on the various live-action sets, Weta Digital was coming to the end of its first official year on *Avatar*, a year of rigorous research and development. But visual-effects producer Eileen Moran, visual-effects supervisor Joe Letteri, co-supervisor Stephen Rosenbaum and other Weta Digital principals had been in discussions with Cameron and Landau as far back as 2005, just as the

company was finishing up Peter Jackson's *King Kong*, for which it had achieved remarkably lifelike computer animation of the title character. "What we'd done on *Kong* really lined up with where Jim was going with *Avatar*," Letteri remarked. In fact, Weta had created a 3-D test of computer-generated imagery for *Avatar* using CG forest assets from Jackson's film.

Initial conversations involved, among other subjects, the filmmakers' plan to do image-based facial capture, recording the actor's facial performance with the single small camera mounted to the head rig. Cameron and his team had judged the image-based solution to be potentially far superior to what had been done before.

The marker-based system used on *Polar Express* and other early performance-capture films had some serious limitations. For example, no data could be recorded of the actor's eye movements, since markers could not be put on an actor's eyeballs. That resulted in a lifelessness in the final character on screen because the animators were forced

to guess what the actor's eyes had done, rather than being able to use the actual performance itself. Also, because the tiny glued-on facial markers were so numerous and so tightly spaced, the motion-capture cameras had to be very close to the actors to get a good solve. That limited the size of the capture Volume to about twenty feet across.

The *Avatar* team considered that much too limiting. They would need to shoot scenes with characters running through the Pandoran forest, leaping up and down from branch to branch. A horse could barely turn in such a limited space, let alone gallop and jump, as was needed for the action in *Avatar*. The Volume created for *Avatar* was six times the size of previous Volumes, with room to run, leap, gallop, and stage the epic battle action of the finale. And with the head-rig system, combined with Giant Studio's powerful biometric solve, it was possible to keep the reference camera operators close to the actors, working right with them in the Volume.

Another major limitation of the old marker-based system was that there was no way to see the actor's performance on the CG character immediately. But with the video from the head rig, the kabuki mask technique was possible, which allowed Cameron to see his actors talking and emoting during the CG camera sessions, rather than waiting many months to see the final CG characters animated.

The advantages were obvious to everyone on the production, but the fact was that no one had ever done it. Weta would be tasked with deriving all their facial performance data from the head rig. This meant that they would have to do a lot of testing and development to create a new type of facial animation pipeline. One question remained to be resolved. Would the head rig have one camera, or multiple cameras? In Cameron's original concept of the head rig, back in 1995, there would be two cameras, one in front and one ninety degrees to the side, to triangulate the data. And the CG animators wanted the extra data from a second camera.

But as *Avatar* ramped up, Cameron became convinced that a single camera was the answer. For one thing, the side camera would hit the actor's shoulder every time he tilted his head, seriously restricting movement. Additionally, the second camera boom would further block the reference cameras, which would often struggle to see past a single boom during actual production.

"Normally, to reconstruct things properly and get really good imagery, you want to have at least two cameras," explained Joe Letteri, "but two cameras on the actor would have created another set of restrictions, having to do with synchronizing data and blocking parts of the face. So we set as our goal a way to make it work with the single camera."

Early in 2006, Letteri and his team at Weta Digital kicked off a six-week project to determine how imagery garnered from the single-camera facial-capture rig might be used to create a completely believable, nuanced facial performance in a CG character. The visual-effects artists procured one of the helmet-camera units from Glenn Derry and proceeded to do their own real-time facial-capture test, capturing stunt performer Shane Rangi, a veteran of the *Lord of the Rings* trilogy, with the single camera. Weta Digital then tracked that performance to a CG character—not a CG avatar or Na'vi, as those digital assets were still a long way from being realized, but a CG head of actor Andy Serkis. "We just happened to have that CG Andy Serkis rigged and ready to go for another project," explained Joe Letteri. From that test, the Weta crew determined that they could create expressive facial animation even from the slightly limited data captured from a single camera perspective.

As *Avatar*'s virtual production commenced at Playa Vista, Weta Digital committed itself wholeheartedly to the project, initiating development of the tools it would need to transform the Los Angeles production's video-game-resolution shots into the most beautifully animated, photorealistic CG shots ever achieved for a film.

Letteri and his team first thoroughly reexamined current CG techniques and tools, many of which had been developed in the early days of computer graphics, devised as shortcuts to deal with computers that had little power or memory. Despite the increased speeds and memory capacities of the computers that followed, some of those shortcuts had remained in place—adapted and modified, to be sure, but still more or less predicated on the limitations of 1980s-era computers.

The result of that wholesale reexamination at Weta Digital was to replace a pipeline that relied too heavily on cheats and shortcuts to emulate reality with a pipeline that was more physically based. "We realized that, in the long run," said Joe Letteri, "to create a world that looks real, it is best to just make it real to begin with." As part of that philosophy, Weta built computer models for Jake, Neytiri, and all of the leading Na'vi and avatar characters with anatomically accurate muscles. Previously, computer

characters' "muscles" were really more like digital balloons positioned beneath CG skin, programmed to inflate and deflate with the movement of the underlying skeletal structures. For *Avatar*, Weta modelers built geometries that simulated real muscles, fat, and skin. This re-creation of real physiology made for a more labor-intensive modeling effort at the beginning, but it would produce far more believable animated characters in the end. "Rather than just faking the movement of all of that underlying muscle and bone with the movement of the surface skin," said Jon Landau, "they were really creating all of that underlying movement. They were working from the inside out, rather than from the outside in—and that took a long time."

Nothing was more critical to the ultimate success of the CG characters than their facial animation. It had been the single-most worrisome issue from the earliest stages of the project. Weta Digital's facial-animation rigs would have to be extremely robust and sophisticated, able to extrapolate from the limited field of view of a single head-rig camera the full range of any given facial expression.

Cameron had believed from the beginning that going to great pains to capture volumes of data from an actor's face was a waste of time and effort, because no matter how dense that data, it *still* wouldn't fully capture the literally thousands of infinitesimal details that make up human expression. It was much more important to account for all the tiny interactions of the many facial muscles with one another, with layers of fat, and with connective tissue and skin. It was what was happening below the surface that had to be understood—not what was at the surface. This realization introduced a sea change in the creation of CG characters, shifting the emphasis from the capture data to "the rig." Only the rig would account for all that subsurface anatomy and interaction. "You could scan the face from the outside all day long and never be able to reproduce those things," Cameron said. "The *rig* is the thing."

It would take Weta a very long time to build those facial rigs, as it was an incremental process of breaking down "chunks" of movement into ever smaller, nearly imperceptible pieces. For the filmmakers, waiting out that long and meticulous process required tremendous patience and faith, both of which were sorely tested when Cameron saw the first facial animation for Jake's avatar. "It was horrible," Cameron recalled, "and I thought, 'Oh my God, we've done everything right, and this is what it looks like?'" Joe Letteri assured Cameron that the animation was the result

of a rig that was only 50 percent complete, and that there were many fine adjustments to be made. He promised him that it would get better.

Letteri knew, from the experience with Gollum and later King Kong, that CG characters that aspire to photo-reality take time to come to life. It was not a magic wand process, but an iterative one that required great patience and experience on the part of the animators. Most critical was their ability to observe the actors, and deeply understand how their faces worked at a neuromuscular level, and how their faces expressed the subtlest nuances of their inner emotional states. With that understanding, and by a series of microscopic adjustments, they could fine-tune the CG faces to behave exactly as the actors' had done.

Weta Digital also devised streamlined, more physically based ways to light *Avatar*'s CG scenes, many of which would consist of literally thousands of CG elements. Through new global illumination techniques, the computer could detect the precise source of lighting in a scene. "For any given point on a surface," said digital-effects supervisor Dan Lemmon, "it would tell us where the light hitting that surface was coming from, and light the object accordingly." Visual-effects supervisors Eric Saindon and Guy Williams were key to implementing the new lighting techniques.

One major lighting problem was how to simulate the look of translucent flesh in the blue-skinned Na'vi and avatar characters. It was a tricky proposition, as there was no real-world example of such vibrantly colored warm-blooded mammals. From the get-go, then, Weta Digital was attempting to make something that audiences would perceive as quite unnatural—blue-skinned people—look natural.

The pivotal decision was the color of Na'vi blood, which would literally color everything. Cameron's treatment called

OPPOSITE: Moore's face being scanned at Lightstage. Weta Digital used this technique to capture highly accurate skin details for each actor who played a CG character, whether Na'vi or avatar. Everything from pore structure and skin tonality to facial imperfections was recorded; the process created a shadowless texture map of the actor's face. To create photorealistic avatar skin, Joe Letteri felt it was necessary to start with the reality of the actor's skin. Norm's avatar would have all the tiny variations of pigmentation scanned from Moore's skin, with the pigment values turned to shades of blue instead of brown. CG lighting would interact with these textures, as well as with "layers" below the skin, scattering the light internally instead of reflecting it. Values would be assigned for "specularity," the shininess of the actor's skin, which is necessary to simulate skin oils and sweat, but if taken too far made the character look like blue vinyl. Months of research and development were required to come up with the organic-looking blue skin.

ABOVE, TOP: Final shot of Neytiri's determined expression as she is about to kill Jake.

FIGURE 1: Saldana's original performance. It is interesting to note that this was the first shot every captured of a principal actor for *Avatar*.

FIGURE 2: Template with video from Saldana's facial camera projected onto static face geometry, known as the "kabuki face." This was done to see eye and mouth movement in the template images.

FIGURE 3: Animation pass with rough lighting. This is where the expression was "tweaked" by animators until it exactly matched Saldana's performance.

FIGURE 4: High-resolution model with hair and costume simulation. Weta Digital used this white render to assess whether the hair "sim" was behaving realistically, according to the laws of gravity and motion, and was interacting properly with Neytiri's head and body.

in the computer models, and also transferred many of the specific moles and freckles and imperfections on an actor's skin to that actor's CG counterpart.

Another lighting problem that had to be solved was how to create the bioluminescence of Pandora's flora. Despite beautiful design art as a guide, once again, the devil was in the details. It was quickly discovered that if every plant was glowing, it looked washed out and destroyed the nighttime look of a scene. Weta determined that they were going to need to be selective and create "negative" areas. A decision was made that the bark of the trees and roots would not emit light directly, but could be covered, when necessary, by patterns of glowing moss. The masses of the enormous trunks became the negatives needed to create areas of light and dark. In addition, all the minute characteristics of the glowing plants needed to be worked out. How translucent were the leaves? How deep in the tissue of the plant did the glow originate? How did the plants interact with pressure from a passing Na'vi or avatar?

All of these questions and hundreds more needed to be answered in order for the Pandoran forest to come to life. It took months of testing of the luminance and color values of every plant and interaction before the scenes started to feel real, and yet keep their dreamlike quality. It was painstaking and frustrating work, and like the facial rigging, it seemed that it would never get there. But when it did, and the night forest came to life, everyone knew that a corner had been turned. Pandora now existed as an unequivocally real forest world by day, with real living breathing characters, and it transformed at night into a phantasmagorical wonderland. In fact, "phantasmagorical"—defined in the dictionary as "as seen in a dream"—was the word that Rick Carter used to describe it. Much later, at test screenings, it was determined that the favorite scenes in the movie, for audiences young and old, were the dreamlike nighttime forest scenes. All the time and effort paid off.

A twelve-shot scene in which Neytiri spots Jake in the jungle, then raises her bow and aims an arrow at him, was the first template to be turned over by production. Weta

for all the creatures of Pandora, including the Na'vi, to have purple blood, emphasizing their alienness. But when this came up in a discussion with Stan Winston, very early on, Winston's reaction was typically instinctive and decisive. "If you cut your hand, what color is the blood?" he said, "The Na'vi blood should be red, so the audience can identify."

Cameron took that advice to heart, and the red Na'vi blood became the key to making the blue skin look real. The blue was now thought of as a pigment, like the melanin in human skin that creates various shades of brown. The pinkness of the tissue below the pigment would need to show through in various places, in the inside of the mouth, around the edges of the eyelids, and on the palms of hands and feet. The CG team used "subsurface scattering" to show how strong backlight interacted with the red blood in the tissue below the surface of the skin. When the skin and lighting characteristics were properly dialed-in, backlight from the sun would actually transmit through the skin and cartilage of a Na'vi ear, glowing red despite the skin's blue pigment. Many times throughout the film, the ears of Jake, Neytiri and the other characters have an orange glow whenever direct sunlight hits them from behind, just as real people do when backlit by the sun. It was the art of observing these minute, familiar details and incorporating them into the CG lighting that ultimately made *Avatar* so breathtakingly real.

Creating blue skin that looked warm, alive, and real, rather than like the blue plastic of a toy, was a challenge that would have to be tackled anew for every scene and every new lighting scenario. Ultimately, the crews would find that integrating many small imperfections in the skin—such as those that appear at a microscopic level even in the most porcelain and creamy of complexions—was one of the keys to creating realistic blue flesh. Weta Digital artists studied pore textures and the irregular distribution of pigment in extreme close-up photographs of crew members to re-create textures

Digital artists and technical leads used those twelve shots to develop methodologies for building their facial rigs—in this case, for Neytiri—as well as for creating the look of the characters and their environments, for lighting, and for everything else that they would need to produce *Avatar*'s final shots.

Fourteen months would pass from the time production turned over that template in February 2007 to the time Weta delivered its first high-resolution shot. Not surprisingly, the filmmakers back in Southern California experienced some excruciating moments during those fourteen months, as they waited to see if Weta Digital would come through, if all of their very high expectations would be met.

"When we finally got back that first scene," recalled Jon Landau, "we got very excited about what Weta had done. In the intensity of Neytiri's eyes, the flare of her nose, in every detail, we could see what Zoë the actress was thinking in that moment. So we said, 'Yeah, this can really work!' But then we got terrified, because we realized we still had 1,900 shots to go." Turnaround times

OPPOSITE: Jake shooting at the attacking thanator while ducking inside the root system of a Pandoran tree.

ABOVE: Frame grab of the same moment.

shortened somewhat as production progressed, but even then, nine months often would pass from the time virtual production turned over a template scene to the time Weta delivered its final version. "It was an interesting coincidence that it was the same length of time that it takes to birth a child. It just took a long time to get each of those character shots to where they needed to be."

New Zealand's summer was turning to autumn when the *Avatar* crew left in March 2008 to return to Los Angeles, where winter was turning to spring. The heavy lifting for the actors and the production crews was over, but it was just starting for Weta Digital, which would produce more than two thousand dynamic and impeccably photorealistic computer-generated shots over the next twenty-three months.

FIVE

UNILTÌRANTOKX: AVATAR

In the old days of studio filmmaking, the mostly unknown and unsung men and women who created visual effects for films were referred to as "the trick department." It was an apt term, and one that so delighted James Cameron, he had considered adopting it when he cofounded the visual-effects facility that came to be known as Digital Domain. By January 1, 2008, *Avatar*'s own trick department, Weta Digital, was deeply into official shot production, regularly video-conferencing with Cameron in Los Angeles via high-speed lines.

In the previous two years, the New Zealand effects team had developed a pipeline and a workflow for producing final shots, which started with the arrival at Weta Digital of the virtual-production template—the video-game-resolution version of a shot, complete with Cameron's final camera work, low-resolution CG characters driven by the actors' captured performances, low-resolution environments, and effects. Edited and tweaked to represent *exactly* the final shot Cameron wanted to see, the template was Weta Digital's bible for a shot. "Even though the scene in the template wasn't at the photoreal level," noted Richie Baneham, "the narrative and emotional context were there, and it all played very clearly and truly. By having a template of the scene for Weta to reference, we maintained consistency in the performances, right down to the smallest detail and idiosyncrasy."

The template's first stop was Weta Digital's layout department, where all of its disparate elements—the often hundreds of separate environmental

OPPOSITE: Jake, as Toruk Macto, leads the gathered Na'vi clans as they prepare for the final battle. Banshee-mounted warriors fly in behind him.

and character digital assets—were pulled apart and lined up to high-resolution versions. More often than not there were disparities between the two, problems resulting from the quick-and-dirty nature of the virtual-production process. Contact points between characters and environments weren't always dead-on, for example, or trees in the environment were scaled improperly.

All of those irregularities were corrected in the initial layout process at Weta, and then the shot was passed on to Weta animation director Andy Jones, Weta codirector David Clayton, and their team of forty-five animators. After tweaking the overall body movement generated by the performance-capture data, the animators turned to the facial animation, which would demand their most intense and meticulous attention.

Over the course of many months, Jones and facial-rigging lead Jeff Unay built muscle-based facial rigs that could be driven by psychologist Paul Ekman's Facial Action Coding System (FACS). Ekman had developed the system from his theory, documented in a number of academic papers and books, that human facial expressions have universal meanings, and that facial muscles could be encoded numerically to produce those universal expressions. "You can say you want an anger pose," said Jones, "put the right numbers into FACS, and the system knows which muscles to pull."

Creating the facial animation was not merely a numbers game, however, nor merely a matter of plugging facial-capture data into a CG character's model. Every close-up shot, in particular, required the eye and the artistry of an animator. "There was still a lot of work to do," said Richard Baneham. "Some of the fundamental legwork was taken out through facial capture, but [all] of those close-ups were beautifully animated pieces of art."

The animators' one overriding goal in the close-ups was to match, *exactly*, the original actor's performance. "If it was a close-up of Sam Worthington, for example," said Andy Jones, "we had to match every detail of his performance, which we didn't get automatically from the facial capture. That's where the animator came in. The animator recognized the details that were missing and put them in. It was that last 10 percent [of keyframe animation] that made it real."

The single small camera on the head rigs, due to its wide lens and proximity to the actor's face, produced imagery that was distorted, creating a kind of fish-eye-lens view of the actor's face. As a result, the imagery from the head-rig camera, though critical to the facial capture, was of little use as reference for the animators. Instead, they used the HD camera footage from the stage as their standard for matching performances. "We always went back to the HD camera reference," said Jones, "which was usually set up at a similar angle to the close-up that Jim wanted

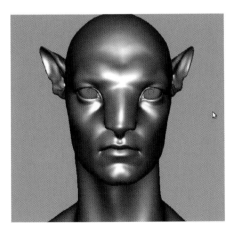 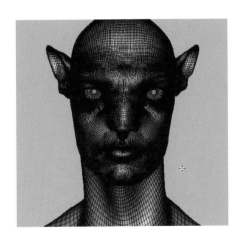 

Avatar has many close-up dialogue shots between its digital characters. Andy Jones's animation aided the Weta Digital facial team in dissecting what FACS (Facial Action Coding System) shapes were blending well with one another—and which ones weren't—as well as deciding if areas of the face were moving enough during speech (mainly the cheek area).

ABOVE: The resolution of the face models were higher polygon counts than Weta has ever used previously. This allowed the Weta facial team to add in the finest of details of skin pores and imperfections, but it came with a price. The character facial pipeline had to be built from the ground up to accommodate the billions of polygons running through the system, as well as the thousands—not hundreds—of facial shapes per character.

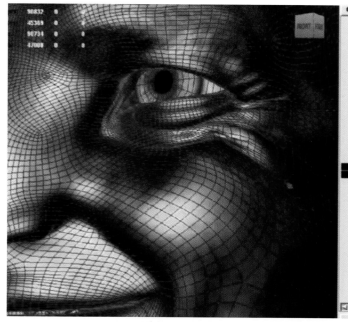

LEFT: The facial animation control set within the software is based primarily on FACS but is not limited to it. The motion-capture artists and animators would do the large majority with the FACS-based controls but then continue finessing their work with a "tweak" set of controls designed specifically to reposition parts of the face. The shape of the opening of the mouth and eyes, for example, had to match the facial references exactly, per shot; this required a significant amount of "hands-on" care. This kind of detailed attention is what the process demanded in order to successfully translate these CG characters into realistic, emotionally driven performances within a fully CG environment.

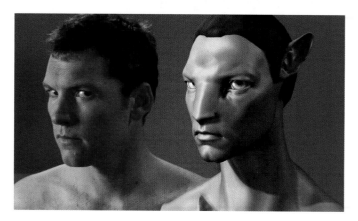

ABOVE: Getting Worthington's stare translated onto Jake's avatar required many iterations. The area that required the most redesign was the eye shape of the digital model in order for it to more closely match Worthington's. Once Weta Digital made this change, it was easier to match the actor's intentions onto Jake's avatar, and thus faithfully—digitally—reproduce his performance in the virtual environment.

ABOVE: Eye looks and head turns were the beginnings of many side-by-side comparisons between Worthington and his avatar character. WD soon progressed into matching static emotional states. For example, the intensity of the rage expression was increased by dialing in new neck muscle and forehead vein controls found in the animation software.

in the film. We'd adjust the performance capture from the head rig to fit the HD performance. Sometimes we had to offset it or tweak the expression a little bit to make it feel right, because the camera that was doing the facial capture had captured the movement of the skin, but not the actor's emotional level or feeling. Comparing that facial capture to the HD camera in the scene, we could see where we needed to push and pull things to make it look more like the actor." Animators "pushed and pulled things" via inputs on slider controls, which enabled them to dial in hundreds of minute facial movements to create a nearly limitless range of expression.

Cameron's fantasy at the outset had been that the facial capture process would be automatic, completely hands-off from the animators. He didn't want the animators embellishing or interpreting the actors' performances. As a director, he wanted to work with the actors as tirelessly as necessary on the set to get the performances perfect, and then not have to deal with the performance again in the animation stage. But that degree of automation proved impossible. The head-rig data could not drive the rigged models one hundred percent. And even if it could, the *characters* were not the *actors*. "Jake's avatar had a broad leonine nose, a protruding muzzle, oversized eyes, and other

features that were different enough from Sam's face that the expressions did not translate perfectly, no matter how much data was captured," Cameron commented. Cameron had to adjust his perception of the process as time went on, and embrace the role of the animator. Finally he was satisfied that through a combination of capture technology and animation artistry, the performances of the actors were being preserved without loss or embellishment, and the "soul" of the performance was intact.

The high-water mark for facial animation was the scene in which Jake confesses that he has been sent to infiltrate Neytiri's Na'vi clan and report back to Colonel Quaritch. Betrayal, hurt, and anger all had to play across Neytiri's face, just as they had on Zoë Saldana's the night

the virtual-production team had shot the scene in Playa Vista. Crews had witnessed one of those rare magic-in-a-bottle moments that night, as the intense emotion and connection between the actors filled the empty stage with a palpable energy.

Some of the most thrilling and anxiety-provoking moments for the teams in both Wellington and Los Angeles were when Weta first revealed a finished shot. After photography ended for the day at Playa Vista, Cameron, Landau and a small group repaired to a dark viewing room and teleconferenced with the crew in Wellington, who were just starting their day. As each shot was unveiled, the tiniest detail would provoke long discussions of how it could be improved. How light played on a flower, sap

dripped, or a tree branch twisted, could consume hours. The scene where Jake's betrayal is revealed to Neytiri was so crucial that Baneham, Jones, and Clayton avoided showing Cameron the animation until they were absolutely certain that they had nailed it. And when Cameron finally saw the computer-animated shots, he felt a rush of relief. If Weta could re-create that scene, he knew, they could do any scene. Of all of *Avatar*'s many "firsts" and achievements, the artful creation of evocative, emotion-driven facial performances was, in Cameron's view, the film's single greatest accomplishment. "A lot of it was due to the character rigs," Cameron said, "which really came a long way. Maybe only 10 percent was keyframe animation, but that 10 percent gave us the fine nuances of expression."

Body animation was less of an issue than facial animation, and would have been even *less* of an issue had the Na'vi and avatars been more fully clothed. But given the skin-revealing nature of Na'vi attire, the animators spent a lot of time ensuring that the body dynamics, as seen in the actors' and stunt doubles' performances on the stage, translated onto the Na'vi musculature. "We were seeing every single muscle movement," said Andy Jones, "every piece of skin movement. [Characters'] muscles had to flex when they were tense, and then relax when they weren't tense. A character might be standing in a pose with his arm out, and we had to figure out if, based on that pose, they were flexing the muscle in that arm or not. We had to figure out which leg they were taking the weight on as they stood

OPPOSITE: Jake confesses and asks for forgiveness from Neytiri (frame grab).

LEFT and ABOVE: Side-by-side comparison of Neytiri and Saldana's original performance, a useful technique in making sure the emotional beats are being hit.

ABOVE: Frame grab from the scene in which Neytiri charges toward Quaritch for the climactic clash of nature against machine, her thanator and Quaritch's AMP suit battling to the death (film export from Weta Digital).

OPPOSITE: Neytiri aiming at Quaritch for the bow shot that saves Jake's life and ends the Colonel's reign of terror (frame grab).

there, and how much that leg muscle might be flexing. We had to decide how much strain you would see in the neck as they were talking or screaming. A lot of that fine detail couldn't be captured in the performance capture, but it had to be there in the characters." Weta Digital's Dana Peters developed a computer simulation to move the skin in a natural manner as each muscle flexed or relaxed. After running that simulation, the animators would then go in with hand controls to adjust and fine-tune the flex of muscles and skin movement as needed.

Weta Digital took a similar approach to creating the movement of leathery skin over musculature for Pandora's creatures. Although the virtual-production team had shot performers as creatures to capture motion data relating to overall movement and blocking in a shot, the animation of the creature itself had to be created from scratch. The creatures of Pandora, unlike the Na'vi and avatar characters, were animated using key-frame CG animation. "This is where the Weta animators, who are among the best in the world, got to really break free, creatively," said Cameron.

The animators' first task was to develop six-limbed walk and run cycles. Before committing to the idea, in fact—very early in *Avatar*'s development—Rob Powers had done internal proof-of-concept tests of the idea. Subsequently, Cameron had enlisted Paul Kavanagh, an animator from Industrial Light & Magic, to develop six-legged animation cycles to ensure the creatures' movement would not look awkward and ungainly. Among Kavanagh's animation cycles was that for the viperwolf. "That test showed the viperwolf moving in a stalking crouch," recalled Cameron, "in what we called the 'ant walk,' a gait in which each pair of legs opposed the motion of the pair ahead of it—walking like an ant. It then speeds up and 'transitions' to what we called the 'coupled gait,' in which the forward pair and the middle pair of legs function together, no longer opposed. This was convincing, and led to the idea that the four forward legs would be grouped more closely,

not evenly spaced along the body, and would sometimes function together, at a gallop or full run, and other times would be opposed." This same principle was applied to all the six-limbed animals.

Weta animators also conducted motion studies shortly after coming onto the project, through which they determined that the best procedure for producing natural, graceful six-legged walk and run cycles was to hide the extra set of middle limbs when executing the first animation pass, establishing a basic walk or run with only four legs. The animator would then copy the animation of the front legs onto the middle legs, slightly offsetting the timings of the leg pairs. "We offset the back legs a few frames back, and offset the forward legs a frame or two forward," explained Andy Jones. "It worked pretty seamlessly. For the direhorse, for example, we developed a gallop cycle, just slightly offsetting the legs so you'd get this cascading effect that still felt like a horse stride."

"The forelegs didn't all hit the ground at the same time," added Cameron, "which gave the creatures a more organic look. The skeletons were adjusted a number of times, both in the design phase and later during animation, to create clearance between the forelegs and the second pair. This applied especially to the shoulder structure, which was adjusted so that the number one foot hit the ground just inside the contact point of the number-two foot. These temporal and spatial adjustments allowed for a highly plausible six-legged motion that appeared perfectly natural."

Though the extra limbs tended to disappear in a blur in running shots, they were evident in the shots in which a creature was standing still. Animators had to devise behaviors and movements for the extra legs in such shots to ensure that these appendages didn't look useless or superfluous. The hammerhead titanothere has a long stationary scene when it first confronts Jake in the forest, for example, and to keep the creature "alive" in the scene, David Clayton created bull-like mannerisms, animating the hammerhead to kick up dust, shift its weight, and stomp the ground with its front leg just before it charges.

Nature reference would provide a real-world basis for all the creature animation, and was often presented to Cameron as a picture-in-picture, running alongside final animation. For the viperwolf, the animators referenced footage of foxes, cheetahs, wolves, and greyhounds. Reference of the racing dogs was particularly useful, as the viperwolves had similarly thin bodies and elongated legs. Animators created more catlike behavior in shots of the predators hunkering low to the ground, on the prowl, but little of that behavior made it into the final film.

The thanator was more feline in its movements, and so the animators looked at reference photos of lions and other big cats. For the scene in which the thanator chases Jake through the forest, production provided Weta's animation team with performance capture of Jake running through, around, and over a series of obstacles. Mirroring the timing of that action, the animators developed the thanator's side of the chase. "Jim gave us that mocap as a kickoff, and then he let us run wild with that chase," recalled Jones. "That was a lot of fun for the animators."

When stunt man Reuben Langdon ducked in the performance-captured part of the chase, for example, the animators would animate a swipe of the thanator's claws to correspond to Langdon's action. And where Jake was knocked sprawling by a big padded "kill stick"—wielded by Garrett Warren—the animators had the thanator tackling him to the ground.

Once the thanator was added, Cameron went back and shot virtual cameras on the final animation. This was a new wrinkle in the production process. Now the capture was going to Weta, not in the form of a completed template,

ABOVE: Cameron and Letteri (Weta Digital Supervisor).

OPPOSITE: Cameron shooting a shot in which the Valkyrie "dorsal gunners" are attacked. Stunt gunners fired at target dots on the green screen, where Na'vi riding banshees would later be added by Weta.

OPPOSITE, TOP: Quaritch draws the AMP suit's meter-long knife and squares off against Neytiri's thanator. In this shot, and several others, Quaritch is a highly accurate "digi-double" using Stephen Lang's captured—not photographed—performance (frame grab).

OPPOSITE, BOTTOM LEFT: Lang taking Winston Studio's AMP Suit gloves for a test drive (on set in New Zealand, mid-October 2007).

OPPOSITE, BOTTOM RIGHT: Cameron shoots Lang as they complete the last pieces of the AMP Suit fight puzzle: the live-action coverage of Quaritch in the cockpit (April 2009, back at Playa Vista).

ABOVE: Frame grab of the Quaritch-driven AMP Suit after his radical escape from the crashing and burning Dragon. Fluid dynamics fire "sim" effects were overseen by John Knoll of ILM.

LEFT: Stan Winston, longtime collaborator and friend to Cameron, in front of the AMP Suit his studio built.

Movement studies began in mid-2006—here (**ABOVE, TOP**) Cameron and Landau describe the virtual production process to FOX's head of physical production, Joe Hartwick. **BOTTOM RIGHT**: Richie Baneham, the production's head of animation, in the Volume at Playa Vista. **BOTTOM LEFT**: Baneham puppets a 1/48th-scale banshee model while movement coach Terry Notary performs the wing movements, to create a combined creature performance in real time. **OPPOSITE**: Weta added minute details of animation to the captured motion to bring the flying creatures to life (frame grab).

OVERLEAF: Editor John Refoua, Baneham, and Cameron reviewing edits, on the live-action set at Playa Vista, during pickup photography (late April 2009).

but as a "spine" for the animation, and then coming back as completed animation to be shot virtually and turned back over to Weta, this time as a finalized template. This added a loop to the pipeline, but it proved to be the way many of the scenes involving creature animation would be done later in the film, including the final battle between Quaritch, Neytiri, and Jake.

For the banshees, animators developed flight maneuvers and a variety of nesting and fighting behaviors in a series of motion studies. Flight animation included moves in which the creature would rise vertically, much like the film's rotorcraft, and then accelerate forward at incredible speed. While basic flapping motions and general flight paths were guided by the motion capture that James Cameron and Richard Baneham had recorded early in production, more specific flight animation was determined by the structure of the creature's four wings, which was similar to the ribbed membrane of a bat's wing. Dana Peters's team was responsible for simulating how that skin membrane would move as the banshee flapped its wings. "[The creatures team] also ran a muscle simulation," said Jones, "so every time the banshee flapped its wings, it kind of strained its chest muscles."

Just as marine organisms inspired the look of many of Pandora's creatures and plants, they served as reference for some of the creature animation. The animation of the wood sprites that land on Jake during his first conversation with Neytiri, for example, was based on the motion of jellyfish, combined with the idea of dandelion seeds dispersing on a breeze. "Jim gave us very specific notes on how he wanted the wood sprites to move," Jones related. "Water is more viscous than air, and so they would move a bit quicker than a jellyfish in water, but they could also move in a way that a dandelion couldn't. So it was a mix between the two."

As the animators were bringing life to the film's creatures and characters, another team of artists at Weta Digital was focused on creating CG Pandora environments in lush photographic detail. Early on, Joe Letteri and Cameron had discussed just how much of the Pandora jungle should be computer generated. Weta had shot most of its *King Kong* jungles using practical models, with some live-action plates thrown in, and Cameron's own inclination at the time he'd first conceived *Avatar* had been to shoot live-action jungles. Just about every live-action film featuring computer-animated characters made in the previous decade had inserted its CG characters into live-action plates—Michael Bay's

Transformer robots and Peter Jackson's Gollum had all lived mostly within a live-action world.

The look of all-CG environments would be limited only by the artists' imaginations, and CG environments would also afford Cameron complete control and flexibility in assembling any given scene. It could be misty or overcast or sunny. It could be day or night, twilight or dawn. Anything was possible in CG, and Cameron felt certain it was the best way to go—*if* Weta Digital could produce all-CG environments that were completely convincing and photoreal. Cameron asked Joe Letteri and his team to do some CG jungle tests early on. "Jim and I met with Joe Letteri and Eric Saindon in New Zealand," recalled Jon Landau. "It was during this meeting that Eric presented the first photorealistic plant environments. Although they had rendered only a small section of forest, it was a proof of concept for the methodology Weta would use for the larger environments." The test convinced the filmmakers that Weta Digital could meet the CG-forest challenge, especially given their long lead time.

Invaluable to the Weta artists in re-creating the rain forest in CG was the HD footage that Cameron and second unit director Steve Quale had shot in Hawaii prior to the shoot in Playa Vista. By studying that reference footage, the Weta effects team was able to see the natural lighting on foliage and characters, such as the subtle interplay of bluish skylight with direct sun, and the way in which sunlight would pass through leaves to light up their undersides, dubbed "transmission" by the Weta lighting artists.

"Creating realistic CG environments and characters requires, first and foremost, a rigorous discipline of observing nature," said Cameron. "So many things that the eye and brain take for granted in real-world experience must be minutely studied, understood and deconstructed, and ultimately reverse-engineered in the sterile, mathematical pseudo-reality of the computer. The artist needs to understand intimately the way different surfaces, whether skin, leaves, rock or water, interact with different types of light . . . soft, diffuse, direct. Strong sunlight on skin will reflect, as well as be absorbed, and retransmitted subcutaneously, called 'sub-

surface scattering.'" Code had to be written to reproduce those subtle effects in CG, otherwise the end result—no matter how detailed the model—would look false.

To build up all-CG environments for their final shots, Weta Digital created high-resolution versions of every low-resolution digital environmental asset in the virtual-art department's library—every tree, plant, bush, flower, and blade of grass. Weta's high-res elements numbered in the tens of thousands, and were mixed and matched for each shot to exactly match the digital environments in the template received from production. After replacing every low-res element with its high-res version, Weta would fill out the environments with additional plants and ground cover, either painting them or generating them through a procedural computer program that simulated plant growth.

One of the most evocative and important settings in the film, featured in two hundred of Weta's shots, is the Tree of Souls, which glows with bioluminescent splendor in night scenes. How to handle the bioluminescence of Pandora's plant life was a topic of much discussion from the earliest concept-art stage to Weta's development of the look in its final shots. An early consideration at Weta was when and how to introduce the "biolume" effect during Jake's night alone in the forest, without distracting from the story. Weta had experimented with shots in which the biolume would suddenly appear, as if by the flip of a light switch. Other tests amped it up very gradually.

Cameron's goal was to introduce the biolume in a manner that would have the most dramatic impact. "We didn't want to give it away immediately," said Robert Stromberg, "and so Jim did something smart, which was to have Jake light a torch just as it starts to get dark. We play a whole scene torch-lit, so you don't give away the bioluminescence, and then Neytiri throws the torch in a river, and it is almost like opening the door to Oz. The torch goes out, and you see the bioluminescence for the first time. It's a beautiful moment of the movie, the moment where we finally get it that the planet isn't evil and bad. It's actually very beautiful."

The floating mountains, held aloft by Pandora's powerful magnetic field, were another beautifully surreal el-

ement of the alien landscape. To illustrate their floating look, Stromberg and his team of artists had projected artwork onto animated geometry and provided those moving concept pieces to Weta Digital. Weta then re-created the mountains at a much larger scale and higher level of photorealism. "We used the initial sequence where Jake and the hunting party go up into the floating mountains to catch their banshees to figure out the look of the floating mountains," said Weta Digital CG supervisor Dan Lemmon. "We struggled a bit to get these massive rocks to look correct, and so we ended up taking real rocks and laser-scanning them, and built detailed computer rock models that way." Photographs of a mountain range in China—captured by concept artist Steven Messing—also provided reference for the floating mountains. Models built from a combination of those photographs and the laser scans provided the basic rock shapes. Weta then textured them with moss, algae, and other vegetation.

In addition to the Pandora rain-forest settings, Weta Digital extended Rick Carter's live-action Hell's Gate

sets with CG backgrounds, and also re-created the live sets digitally to give Cameron maximum flexibility in regard to camera angles and movement. With *all* of Hell's Gate built in 3-D in the computer, Cameron could literally point his camera anywhere on the virtual-production stage and know that a fully realized, detailed environment for that camera view was available to him; further, through the wonders of Simulcam, he could see a low-res version of that environment, immediately, in his camera viewfinder. The team had also used the virtual camera to scout and block scenes on live-action sets *before* those sets were even built, informing the construction process and guiding the art department as to precisely what would have to be built.

Weta Digital also created high-resolution assets representing Hell's Gate vehicles, aircraft, and other hardware, such as the AMP Suit, which would be seen both in its practical, full-scale form and as a fully computer-generated model. All of the aircraft were modeled and animated to suggest an advanced technology, with rotor systems that

OPPOSITE: Cameron at Playa Vista in April 2009, operates the Fusion 3-D camera on a Technocrane during the final filming.

ABOVE: Jake, attacking during the final battle, grips a bridle he has lashed to the leonopteryx's antennae (frame grab).

enabled the helicopters to take off vertically and hover, but also accelerate at rapidly. Weta conducted early tests of Scorpion, Samson, and Dragon flight animation, all of which would figure prominently in the end battle, a sequence that runs for sixteen minutes and features thousands of animated digital elements.

From the beginning, Cameron had envisioned this climactic confrontation between the Na'vi and the RDA forces as "the mother of all battles." "The battle is aerial," said Cameron, "it's on the ground, it's cavalry, it's hand-to-hand. It's absolutely the biggest thing I've ever done." Ultimately, the end battle was so complex and involved so many CG elements, the filmmakers awarded some of the battle shots to other visual-effects companies as a way to ease the burden on Weta Digital, which was expending most of its resources to finalize its slate of character- and creature-related shots.

The team at Industrial Light & Magic, with whom Cameron had collaborated very successfully on *The Abyss* and *Terminator 2*, took on close to two hundred shots, un-

der the expert supervision of John Knoll, a veteran of *Star Wars* Episodes I, II, and III (1999; 2002; 2005), and many other visual-effects-heavy films. "We wanted to help them out in whatever way we could," Knoll recalled, "but we were busy with other things, and so our resources were limited. We knew we'd be able to do more shots if they were relatively similar and used the same assets, and so the sequence that made the most sense for us to do was the end battle, focusing primarily on shots of the aircraft—the Scorpion, Samson, and Dragon. For the most part, those assets were developed at Weta, and we imported them into our system, although we did the texture- and look-development on the Dragon."

ILM imported scene files from Lightstorm, converted them to work in their pipeline, and then refined the flight-path motion from the motion-capture stage. Cameron and Richie Baneham had captured those flight paths holding onto aircraft models and walking the stage, resulting in some bounce in the motion as the men took each step. The ILM team first smoothed out that bounce,

ABOVE: Jake in flight, with war paint (frame grab).

OPPOSITE: Jake attacks the Valkyrie shuttle as it is about to bomb the Tree of Souls. Taking out the gunners with his 30-caliber machine gun, he will next lob fragmentation grenades into the intake of the shuttle's port-forward lift engine, causing the enormous craft to roll violently and lose control, hitting a rock arch and crashing (frame grab).

then developed flight animation according to Cameron's detailed instructions. "Jim was very specific about how he wanted the helicopters to fly," said Knoll, "how big he wanted them in frame, how fast they should move. The upside of these scene files, with all the motion and camera work in them, was that it was a very direct way to communicate all of those things to us. Our job was to keep the helicopter where it was in those scenes, to maintain what it was doing, but give it flight dynamics that looked more realistic."

ILM generated environments for its end battle shots, as well, including the floating mountains, carefully matching those created by Weta. ILM ultimately contributed more than half of the floating mountain shots.

ILM also created the film's opening shot. Even though the opening scenes of the film changed dramatically during the editing, the first shot of the film (as with the last shot of the film) never changed. For a long time, the film had begun on a polluted future Earth, with RDA agents visiting Jake to recruit him into the avatar program. Late in the cutting process, Cameron decided to begin the story in space, with Jake's journey already in progress, and reveal that back-story in flashbacks.

But the film was always intended to open with a dream image, flying over a misty, primeval landscape. "It was to be an ambiguous image that could be Earth or could be Pandora," Cameron explained, "but an image that would, along with the voice over, introduce the idea of a man's personal journey, a journey as much of mind as of place." To maintain the ambiguity, ILM created foliage that didn't look too alien from that which could be found on Earth. The shot was a significant challenge: to create a CG landscape that the audience would accept as fully photographic, and to sustain it for many seconds. It was the first shot of the movie and it had to be seamless. ILM was ultimately able to create that unassailable sense of reality, but the final version of the shot took three weeks to render on their "render wall," one of the biggest rendering facilities in existence.

ILM created other views of Pandora, including the landing sequence in which the Valkyrie shuttle flies over the vast open pit mine, and we see the enormous machines tearing open the ground to extract unobtainium. After that,

the shuttle approaches Hell's Gate and we see the layout of the base for the first time. ILM's part of the scene ends with the shuttle settling to the ground on its massive landing gear in a blast of jetwash.

"John Knoll and his crew at ILM did a fantastic job of creating all of these shots for us," noted Jon Landau. "They had to reach the very high standards of photorealism and dynamic action set by Weta Digital in the rest of the film—and they did. The artists at ILM are first-rate."

Framestore, a prominent visual-effects company based in the United Kingdom, realized post-landing shots of the bustling tarmac, complete with ambulatory CG AMP Suits. Framestore's initial shot picks up as Jake exits the shuttle in his wheelchair, and was just one of the company's seventy Hell's Gate exteriors and interiors.

Framestore enlivened its 3-D environments with animated aircraft, vehicles, and digital doubles. Similarly, Prime Focus, a Los Angeles–based visual-effects facility, extended

Rick Carter's operations-center set with busy CG backgrounds matted into windows formerly backed by green. Pixel Liberation Front, in Venice, California, contributed graphics for aircraft and AMP Suit displays, while Hybride, in Montreal, created link-room graphics and extended link-room sets digitally for more than one hundred shots. Buf Compagnie (France) executed the link-transfer effect, seen when the human controller's consciousness is transferred to the body of the avatar; Hydraulx (Santa Monica, California) provided set extensions for cryovault and crematoria scenes; and Blur (Venice, California) delivered very high-resolution shots of space for the scene of the Valkyrie shuttle en route to Pandora. Other companies performed general digital fixes, removing wires and rigs from shots where necessary. Visual-effects producer Joyce Cox came onto the show in postproduction to orchestrate and manage the effects shots coming in from all these different vendors.

Even with this outside help, which amounted to about six hundred shots total, the majority of the effects work in *Avatar* remained Weta Digital's. The unprecedented size of the job was such that Weta's CG assets for the film consumed more than one thousand terabytes of digital storage. This made *Avatar* the first motion picture to require more

than a "petabyte" of memory. *Titanic*, by contrast, had required only two terabytes of storage for the digital ship, backgrounds, and passengers, and it had required a special meeting of the board of Digital Domain to okay the purchase of the second terabyte, for one million dollars. A lot had changed in a decade.

By the time Weta met its final delivery date, November 6, 2009, the company had produced 110 minutes of CG animation, slightly more than two-thirds of *Avatar*'s total 162-minute running time, and approximately two thousand visual-effects shots, each of which had to be rendered twice—representing the left- and right-eye perspectives—for the purposes of 3-D.

As he integrated final CG shots from Weta and other vendors, Cameron continued to refine and edit the film, a winnowing process that also clarified where bits of action or narrative were missing. During the last year of production, Cameron shot pickups to fill those holes, as well as shots that had never made it onto the Wellington shoot schedule, at Playa Vista. Among those left to the end of production were shots for the battle scene in which Quaritch, in an AMP Suit, takes on Neytiri (atop a thanator) and Jake.

PREVIOUS SPREAD: Led by Colonel Quaritch, the Valkyrie shuttle, the Dragon, and a bank of Samsons and Scorpions head into the final battle (frame grab).

OPPOSITE: Many of the technologies for making *Avatar* were created from the ground up; so, too, was the editorial process that supported it. Says Rivkin, "Some of these effects sequences were so complicated that I'd sit in front of the screen for a while in an attempt to see how best to go about tackling it." In a unique combination of production and post, the editors began work with Cameron early on, and together, they essentially edited a number of times. First, they would take the selected takes and build a performance edit, then the scenes were broken down and prepped for camera. Cameron would create shots for each scene using a playback of the selected performances, and an initial edit was constructed alongside the editors in the Volume during the virtual camera process; that was later refined and went to Weta and what returned was material for the third pass and the cutting and trimming of the final film. Rivkin further says, "It was a very elaborate process from start to finish, just by the nature of how it was done—selecting performances, building and preparing for virtual camera, and then taking it through a finished template edit; hands down, it was the most complex film I've ever been involved with."

ABOVE: With Toruk Macto no longer needed, the leonopteryx flies home (frame grab).

The complexity arose from the fact that there were five characters in the scene—Jake, Neytiri, the thanator, Quaritch, and his AMP Suit—all performed by human players, all closely interacting with one another. But there were four different scales, and only one of them human. The contacts between characters of different scales, and the seamless blending of live-action elements and CG, made this the most complex sequence that Cameron and his team had ever attempted. "It took us a long time to figure out how to shoot that scene," Cameron said. "We thought it would take us about three months to figure out how to do it. It wound up being a *year* and three months."

To roughly block the scene, Alicia Vela-Bailey performed as the thanator, wearing a Neytiri puppet (about the size of an organ-grinder's monkey) on her back to remind her not to crush Neytiri as she whirled and leaped. Subsequently, she performed Neytiri's action, riding a thanator set piece as crew members moved it violently to and fro, like the mechanical bull in *Urban Cowboy*. The motion-capture system captured the natural movement of her body as she attempted to hold on to the thrashing animal. "Later," Cameron explained, "Weta animators would take the rough blocking and Alicia's raw motion as Neytiri, and combine

LEFT: Cameron and supervising sound editor Christopher Boyes taking a moment to discuss sound design (outside at Playa Vista, April 2008).

OPPOSITE: Wild mountain banshee rookery and part of the floating mountains in the Flux Vortex. Development painting by Cole.

BELOW: In the sound edit room; one month and four days prior to film launch (November 14, 2009).

them using key-frame animation, into one fluid whole."

But that only accounted for half the battle. The AMP Suit proved an even tougher problem to solve—so tough, in fact, that it wasn't figured out for a year after principal photography was complete. It required a separate capture session, in which Cameron shot Kevin Dorman as he performed the AMP Suit. "To make it even more bizarre," said Cameron, "Kevin was matching his timing to Stephen Lang, who was being captured as Quaritch, acting out the major beats of the fight nearby on stage." Through the magic of virtual production, the Quaritch character was made to appear inside the AMP Suit, as if he was driving its movements. Later, this combo was shot in a virtual camera session, to create shots of Quaritch operating the AMP Suit in the fight.

The captured motion of the AMP Suit was used to program a hydraulic motion-base, which then moved the real, full-size Winston AMP Suit during live-action photography against a green screen. "For these shots," said Cameron, "Stephen Lang returned to play the scene again, this time for actual photography. The motion-base slammed and whirled the AMP Suit, and Stephen went along for the ride, acting in sync with the movement so that it appeared he was moving the suit, instead of vice versa."

Glenn Derry and his team provided the motion base, programming it to repeat the AMP Suit moves Cameron had captured with the stunt performer in the motion-capture Volume. To allow Cameron better camera access inside the AMP Suit, the Winston crew removed the arms for some setups, and then visual-effects artists tracked CG arms into final shots.

With the wrap of the pickup shoot in June 2009, Giant Studios' four-year stint on *Avatar* came to an end. It had been the most rewarding experience in the company's history. "It was great to work with Jim, because he has such vast knowledge in computer science and technology in general," Matt Madden commented. "We could communicate to him what our capabilities were, and he would clearly understand and push it to its limit. If there was a technical issue, you could explain it to him, and he would understand what you were saying. That was one of the most rewarding parts of working on *Avatar*."

Throughout that summer, Cameron and Landau screened the film—still a work in progress—for a select

few friends and former colleagues, such as *The Hurt Locker* (2008) director Kathryn Bigelow, visual-effects supervisor Rob Legato, and visual-effects supervisor John Bruno. Also in attendance were visual effects artists Robert and Dennis Skotak, whom Cameron had known from the earliest days of his career at Roger Corman's studio. "We invited them to join us for this internal screening," recalled Jon Landau. "And then that was followed by a conversation to find out what they thought."

For subsequent screenings at Lightstorm—and even later at Fox, when the film was nearer completion—audience members filled out traditional preview cards, answering specific questions as to which characters and scenes worked or didn't work, and why. "We got some very valuable feedback from those cards," Landau said, "and we learned that there were things we thought were obvious, which weren't so obvious to other people. For example, someone said it wasn't clear that the Na'vi only had four digits on their hands. There was a whole scene where Sigourney's character holds up her fingers and the Na'vi kids laugh, because she has more fingers than they do. That scene made sense to us, but it didn't make sense if you didn't know that the Na'vi only have four digits."

The preview screenings also revealed something neither Cameron nor Landau had ever remotely considered: During the love scene between Jake and Neytiri in the willow glades, they had originally sealed their bond by connecting the neural fibers of their queues—just as we had seen Jake do earlier while learning to ride a direhorse and when claiming his banshee in the rookery. Inevitably, the action elicited nervous laughter from the screening audience. "It had never occurred to us that the audience would feel uncomfortable with them connecting their queues at the end of that sequence," said Landau. "But the reaction was universal. I think it was just a bridge too far. Whatever it was, it got an audible giggle and was noted in most of the cards."

In addition to discovering what worked and didn't work in the film, the preview screenings helped the filmmakers to determine where it could be cut for length. "We knew it was going to be a long movie," said Landau, "but we needed to get rid of the word *too* in front of *long*. That wasn't something we could necessarily judge, and that's why it was so important to go through that screening process." Cameron, working with editors Stephen Rivkin and John Refoua and first assistant editor Jason Gaudio, had been editing the film all along, cutting performance-cap-

ture scenes to precise lengths so that Weta Digital would have an accurate template of the scene from which to work. At this postproduction stage, the editors looked for parts of scenes—and even entire sequences—that could be cut, to make the movie as lean as possible without losing any of its narrative impact.

Another major task completed during the six-month period between the wrap and the film's December release was the final sound mix and editing of dialogue, sound effects, and music. Supervising sound editor Addison Teague had been with production throughout, to attend to on-set sound needs and provide creative feedback; supervising sound editor Christopher Boyes had started creating cries and other sounds for the banshees in December 2006, a full two years earlier than he would typically begin on a movie. "It was essential to Jim's editorial process that he have sounds to work with," explained Jon Landau. "Therefore, it was essential that our sound team come on earlier than they would on other shows."

"On this film," Christopher Boyes added, "I knew I had a huge challenge on my hands." To create the audible world of Pandora, Boyes recorded jungles from around the globe, adding to the library of sounds he'd accumulated for jungle scenes in *Jurassic Park III* (2001) and *King Kong* (2005).

For any given scene, Boyes supplied Cameron with a wide selection of sound effects from which he could pick and choose; using those selections, Cameron started building up scenes a solid year before the film's release. Sound effects included a variety of cries, growls, bleats, and other vocalizations unique to the creatures of Pandora. For the banshee, designers came up with a sound vocabulary that would indicate whether the creature was agitated or calm, in an aggressive state or a passive one. Viperwolf vocalizations were inspired by those of coyotes, which Cameron heard on a nightly basis from his secluded home in the Malibu hills. Noting the specific sounds made by the coyotes as they closed in on their prey, Cameron suggested that the designers integrate similar vocalizations in the viperwolf hunting scene. Addison Teague recorded coyotes in Malibu, and the sound team mixed those recorded sounds with hyena vocalizations to create the distinctive sound of hunting viperwolves.

Boyes shared duties with sound re-recording mixers Gary Summers and Andy Nelson, both of whom also started on the film earlier than they normally would have, due to the unusual nature of *Avatar*'s production. With edited template

shots available from the earliest stages of production, the sound team could integrate sound effects and dialogue into a video-game-resolution scene, confident that it represented how the scene would be played and timed in the final cut. "The template was frame-accurate," James Cameron noted, "and it was accurate compositionally, and so, in theory, we could final-mix the movie to the template." In practice, it was not quite so cut-and-dried, because scenes changed in subtle ways as Cameron continued to refine the film. Still, the sound team was able to mix dialogue and sound effects that were more or less final into the template. They also mixed temporary music into template scenes, which helped to define their dramatic rhythms and aided Cameron in the editing process. "Having the sounds available as you're cutting picture actually *influences* how you cut the picture to some extent," explained Cameron.

Gary Summers, who had worked with Cameron on *Terminator 2* and *Titanic,* integrated the film's dialogue into the final sound mix. As much as possible, Cameron wanted to use the dialogue as it had been recorded during the performance-capture sessions, when the actors were really in the moment, working off one another's performances. Production dialogue had been captured by a small micro-

phone mounted discreetly on the camera boom of the head rig. Every actor had his or her own microphone, which resulted in clearer dialogue recordings than what are typically picked up by production mics hanging over a scene.

In a few cases, however, the production sound had been contaminated, either by noise from wind machines or through Cameron's use of the precanned sound effects onstage to help set the mood and action of a scene for the actors. Where actors' dialogue from the stage had been ruined, their lines had to be re-recorded in automated dialogue replacement (ADR) sessions, overseen by supervising sound editor Gwendolyn Whittle. To ensure a closer match between the re-recorded dialogue and the dialogue as spoken by the actors onstage, Cameron had the actors do their ADR to the HD close-up reference recordings of their performances, rather than to their final CG characters.

Dialogue tracks were mixed into even loud action scenes in such a way as to ensure that the characters would be heard clearly. For Cameron, character, not action, was the key to every scene, even the large-scale battle scenes, which he had edited with the same character-centered philosophy in mind. Amid shots of the RDA and Na'vi armies, the flying Samsons and Scorpions, the AMP Suits

ABOVE: Music composer James Horner (*Titanic*) orchestrating a film score. Horner is a longtime friend and former collaborator of Cameron's.

ABOVE: Horner discussing the score with Landau while visiting the set in Wellington (March 2008). A year later, Horner worked with ethnic percussionists in the Volume (OPPOSITE) to capture them playing a circular array of Na'vi drums for the "Battle Prep" scene, which was later taken out of the film.

and myriad creatures on the ground, and the gunfire and explosions, Cameron returned again and again to his main characters to ensure that the audience would always know how Neytiri and Jake, especially, were faring in the battle.

Cameron directed the sound team to mix in character dialogue so that their voices would be clearly heard in the din of battle, as well. Similarly, for the scene in which Jake is chased by the thanator, Cameron asked that the sound of his labored breathing be heard against the cacophony of the thanator's screams, the trampled jungle, and the heart-pounding music. "We would get into the mix," said Gary Summers, "and Jim would say, 'I'm losing my character. I can't hear him breathing. If I can't hear the main character and the threat to him and his panic, then it's just a big monster scene. It's not about the character.'"

Sound re-recording mixer Andy Nelson was primarily responsible for integrating the music score by composer James Horner, who had so beautifully scored Cameron's *Aliens* and *Titanic*. Cameron had used much of Horner's tribal-influenced *Apocalypto* (2006) score as the temp music while cutting and finishing *Avatar*, but Horner delved even more deeply into tribal percussion and other sounds for *Avatar*. In fact, his earliest compositions for the film consisted entirely of tribal instruments and music. At Cameron's suggestion, he incorporated more orchestral music, punctuating it with tribal-inspired percussion, woodwinds, and vocalizations.

During the summer of 2009, Horner and his composing team were bunkered in a house in Calabasas, eating,

sleeping, and breathing the Avatar score. A half-dozen members of the music crew were living the house, and they puzzled over cues starting with their morning pancakes. To protect against piracy, the composers were in lock-down, with a guard stationed at their gate and a padlock on every laptop.

For Horner, music editors Dick Bernstein and Jim Henrikson, and electronic music arranger Simon Franglen, finding the balance between traditional orchestral music and the tribal sounds proved to be among the most challenging aspects of creating the score for *Avatar*; Andy Nelson, though, enjoyed an atypical level of control and flexibility in how he mixed those disparate elements, as Horner and his scoring engineer, Simon Rhodes, had delivered many of these elements to the mix stage on separate tracks.

All of the sound designers and mixers worked to a 2-D version of the final film, but they also had sessions with Cameron in which they would watch the movie in 3-D but without sound, just to take in the stereoscopic experience and note where sound effects and music might enhance that experience. For example, tracer fire that looked fairly flat in 2-D would have more depth and direction in 3-D, and the mixers would adjust the volume and trajectory of the tracer-fire sound effects to support that visual.

With the final scoring of the film in November 2009, *Avatar* was completed. Amid heavy media coverage and fan anticipation, the movie premiered in London on December 10, 2009, and in Los Angeles on December 16, 2009. The film went into wide release around the world in the days that followed. Audience response was unequivocally enthusiastic, and within thirty-nine days, *Avatar* broke the all-time box-office record set by *Titanic*—a record Cameron's prior film had held for twelve years.

Audiences didn't just see *Avatar*; they experienced it. Its high-resolution imagery, scrupulously detailed environments, and artfully realized computer-generated characters, combined with its state-of-the art stereoscopic and large-format IMAX presentation, made *Avatar* the most fully immersive movie ever created. "One of the things we hoped to do with *Avatar* was change the movie-going experience," said Jon Landau. "We didn't want people to walk out of *Avatar*, and say, 'I saw a movie.' We wanted them to say, 'I experienced a movie.' 3-D took away a subconscious barrier that has always been there with the audience, which is the screen plane. Through 3-D, we wanted

to make that screen plane disappear, so that the audience would be looking into a window on a world."

It was a window on a world that was utterly original, fresh, and new. *Avatar*'s characters and settings weren't based on a comic book or a novel or a video game. *Avatar* wasn't a remake of an old fantasy or sci-fi film, nor a tired franchise sequel. It was a story and a universe that sprang from the head of James Cameron, and was then realized through the imaginations of artists and the daring of those willing to position themselves at the vanguard of technology.

Even with the success and critical acclaim of the film, few people really understood that technology and its implications for filmmaking. That fact was driven home when the Academy of Motion Picture Arts and Sciences honored *Avatar* with nine Academy Award® nominations, but did not recognize any of the film's leading actors.

The oversight suggested to Cameron that the Hollywood film community had a long way to go before it would really grasp the performance-capture process and how integral the actor was to what wound up on-screen. F. Murray Abraham and Nicole Kidman had worn prosthetics for their roles as Antonio Salieri and Virginia Woolf in *Amadeus* (1984) and *The Hours* (2002), respectively, and both had won Oscars, because the voters understood that Abraham and Kidman were there, underneath all the latex, driving those performances. Just as surely, Zoë Saldana and Sam Worthington were "underneath" all the ones and zeroes that went into the computer-generated characters of Neytiri and Jake. Creating a character through performance capture is as pure a form of acting as any done before a camera. The only thing missing is the lens. "The acting community needs to understand it before they can embrace it," Cameron said. "And right now, they don't understand it."

Even those actors involved in *Avatar* hadn't understood it entirely when they signed on, but they signed on anyway, putting their faith in James Cameron. The entire

Avatar adventure, in fact, was an exercise in faith—the actors' and the studio's faith in Cameron and Landau, and the filmmakers' faith in their technical teams and the artists at Weta Digital. More than anything else, *Avatar* required faith, on everyone's part, in a new way of making a movie.

"In many ways," admitted Landau, "the naïveté that we had about what it would take to ultimately succeed with this movie enabled us to take those first few steps. Had we known what it would take, we might never have taken those steps. It was really a NASA type of project. When we started, we said, 'Okay, we're going to get to the moon.' In this case, that moon was Pandora, and, thanks to the ingenuity of a lot of people, we got there."

Two months after *Avatar*'s release, the Visual Effects Society, an organization that counts most of the visual-effects artisans in the film industry as its members, honored James Cameron with a Lifetime Achievement Award. In accepting the award, Cameron spoke to the crowd with both passion and humility about the experience of making *Avatar* and what it all meant:

> I've been asked a lot recently in interviews, "What was [your] inspiration for *Avatar*?" and I started thinking back, thinking back, and I wind up slamming all the way back to being seven years old, sitting in the movie theater and seeing *Mysterious Island* and *Jason and the Argonauts* and *The 7th Voyage of Sinbad*—and not knowing how it was done, having no clue, and *not caring*. . . .
>
> Arthur C. Clarke had these laws, and his third law said, "Any sufficiently advanced technology is indistinguishable from magic." Well, to me, when I was a kid, what Ray Harryhausen did was magic. And now, what we're doing is absolute magic to the average person. We could sit down with them for ten hours and try to explain it, and they wouldn't get it. But that's OK. It doesn't matter.

For audiences who were transported by *Avatar*, it's not important to know how the fantastical world of Pandora came to be—it's enough just to visit that world. But there's a magic to this movie even for the thousands of artists and craftspeople who worked on *Avatar*, and for the fans who now know every detail about its creation. That's the magic of venturing into the impossible.

RIGHT: Neytiri, facing certain death, resolves to attack anyway (frame grab).

ABOVE, TOP: Moore, Gerald, Weaver, Lang, Worthington, and Rao.

ABOVE, BOTTOM: Cameron addresses the cast and crew on the first day of principal photography in Wellington, New Zealand (October 23, 2007). The producers were very impressed by the craftsmanship, professionalism, and enthusiasm of the New Zealand crew.

THE MAKING OF

AVATAR